GOLD RUSH FEVER

A STORY OF THE KLONDIKE, 1898

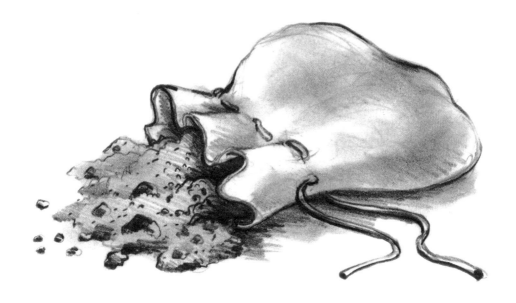

WRITTEN BY BARBARA GREENWOOD
ILLUSTRATED BY HEATHER COLLINS

KIDS CAN PRESS

For Bob, with love — BG
For Graham — HC

Kids Can Press acknowledges the financial support of the Ontario
Arts Council, the Canada Council for the Arts and the Government
of Canada, through the BPIDP, for our publishing activity.

Published in Canada by
Kids Can Press Ltd.
29 Birch Avenue
Toronto, ON M4V 1E2

Published in the U.S. by
Kids Can Press Ltd.
2250 Military Road
Tonawanda, NY 14150

www.kidscanpress.com

Edited by Valerie Wyatt
Designed by Blair Kerrigan/Glyphics
Printed and bound in Hong Kong by Book Art Inc., Toronto

The hardcover edition of this book is smyth sewn casebound.
The paperback edition of this book is limp sewn with a
drawn-on cover.

CM 01 0 9 8 7 6 5 4 3 2 1   CM PA 01 0 9 8 7 6 5 4 3 2 1

Canadian Cataloguing in Publication Data

Greenwood, Barbara, date
    Gold rush fever : a story of the Klondike, 1898
Includes index.
ISBN 1-55074-852-1 (bound)   ISBN 1-55074-850-5 (pbk.)

1. Klondike River Valley (Yukon) — Gold discoveries — Juvenile
literature. I. Collins, Heather. II. Title.
FC4022.3.G743 2001 j971.91'02 C00-933061-5 F1095.K5G743 2001

Photos: Manuscripts, Special Collections, University
Archives/University of Washington Libraries/Photos by E A
Hegg. Page 29: Hegg 98; page 58: Hegg 227; page 79: Hegg 2267;
page 132: Hegg B71; page 154: Hegg 496.

Kids Can Press is a Nelvana company

Acknowledgments

The Klondike Gold Rush, which spanned the years 1896
to 1899, has been well documented. Many stampeders
wrote memoirs or published diaries; in later years,
numerous historians looked back at varying aspects of
the event. For a general overview of this tumultuous
phenomenon in North American history, I am indebted
to Pierre Berton for his detailed and carefully
documented *Klondike, The Last Great Gold Rush, 1896–1899*
(McClelland and Stewart, Revised Edition, 1972) and
most particularly for his photo album *The Klondike Quest:
A Photographic Essay, 1897–1899* (McClelland and Stewart,
1983). Also useful for its reproduction of photographs
was *One Man's Gold Rush: A Klondike Album* by Murray
Morgan (Douglas & McIntyre, 1995).

*Gold Rush, Reliving the Klondike Adventure in Canada's
North* (Gordon Soules Book Publishers, 1996), the story of
the year Ian and Sally Wilson spent following in the
stampeders' footsteps, gave valuable insight into the
physical trials the stampeders would have faced. *Chilkoot
Trail* (Lost Moose, The Yukon Publishers, 1996), by David
Neufeld and Frank Norris, examined in detail the
geography and climate of the region and documented
the stampeders' struggles to cross such difficult terrain.
Frances Backhouse's *Women of the Klondike* (Whitecap
Books, 1995) is a vivid account of the trials and
accomplishments of female stampeders.

Of the many memoirs, diaries and first-person
accounts available, I found particularly useful Tappan
Adney's *The Klondike Stampede* (originally published in
1899, reissued by UBC Press in 1994) and *Faith of Fools,
A Journal of the Klondike Gold Rush* (Washington State
University Press, 1998), William Shape's diary of his
yearlong hunt for gold — recently discovered after a
century in limbo.

I am especially grateful to David Neufeld, Yukon and
Western Arctic Historian, Parks Canada, for his careful
reading of the manuscript and his helpful comments
and suggestions. Thanks are due also to the Kids Can
Press team for their care and concern in the ongoing
scrutiny of the manuscript as it passed through the
production stages.

This book would not have been possible without
Heather Collins's uncanny ability to capture an historical
period with her pencil, my editor Valerie Wyatt's creative
solutions for dealing with an overabundance of material
and, as always, my husband Robert E. Greenwood's
emotional support and tireless researching.

CONTENTS

PROLOGUE

Will you look at this old photo? There's me, all of 13 years old and dressed for the biggest adventure of my life. Was I proud of those high-laced boots! And that's my brother, Roy. Doesn't he look natty in his brand-new stampeder's gear? Who'd ever guess he was burning up with fever.

Gold fever, it was, and I know just when it took him — July 17, 1897. What a morning! Newspaper headlines screaming about a million dollars in gold heading right here to Seattle. Hordes of people rushing for the docks and a ship expected from some godforsaken place up north. Roy and I just had to see it with our own eyes.

One look at those men dragging boxes full of gold nuggets down the gangplank and Roy was a goner. Not that he was alone. In no time, half the country was climbing over the other half to be first on a ship headed north to the goldfields.

I caught a fever that morning, too. Newspaper fever. I'd been working as an errand boy at the *Post-Intelligencer*. One more year of school and I figured they'd take me on as a cub reporter. But then, suddenly, right on my doorstep — the story of the century. I made up my mind that minute — we were going.

Aunt Rachel said we were crazy. Where were we going to get the money? That stopped Roy in his tracks. He'd lost his share of our inheritance in a grocery store that had gone bust.

Well I still had *my* share, and I offered it to Roy — if he'd take me along. At first Roy objected. You're just a kid, he said. Bad enough I lost my own money without losing yours, he said. But I kept at him. The way I saw it, taking a gamble on the goldfields was Roy's only chance to make himself a new grubstake. And me? No way was I missing out on the adventure of a lifetime. No sir!

Fifty years now I've roamed the world as a reporter. Covered some pretty big stories, too. But, in my books, the biggest of them all was my first story — the Klondike Gold Rush of 1897.

The Quest for Gold on the Last Frontier
by Tim Olsen, Special Correspondent
Being an Eyewitness Account of Life in the Klondike Goldfields of the Yukon

September 8, 1897

We're off for the Klondike — real stampeders at last!

What a crowd packed the docks, flinging their hats in the air and cheering wildly as we steamed away on the SS Queen. Even Aunt Rachel was there. It was raining when we started, but the sun came out and then a rainbow. A good omen! We'll find our pot of gold. I just know it.

September 10, 1897

Two days out of Seattle. I wonder what adventures I'll have before I see it again.

I'm on the upper deck, sitting on bales of hay for the horses. They're crowded into stalls down below, poor things, whin̶ ̶ ̶ ̶ ̶ ̶ ̶ ̶ ̶ ̶ ̶ ̶ ̶ ̶ ̶ ̶ ̶bout. I keep Pal on a leash. Roy was dead ag̶ ̶ ̶ ̶ ̶ ̶ ̶ ̶ ̶ ̶ ̶ ̶ ̶ ̶ ̶ ̶y sled dogs will be valuable̶ ̶ ̶ ̶ ̶

̶ ̶de Roy and me
̶nly one bunk
̶ded, and the
̶ uncovered
̶be landing

THE BIG CLIMB

September 10, 1897

Two days out of Seattle. I wonder what adventures I'll have before I see it again. I'm on the upper deck, sitting on bales of hay for the horses. They're crowded into stalls down below, poor things, whinnying and crashing about. I keep Pal on a leash. Roy was dead against me bringing him, but people say sled dogs will be valuable up north, and Pal is good at pulling.

September 13, 1897

Couldn't write the last few days. The rolling and pitching made Roy and me seasick. Most other people, too. What's worse, Roy and I have only one bunk between us, even though we paid for two. The whole ship is overcrowded, and the smell below deck is unbearable, what with people retching and the uncovered chamber pots. So Pal and I sleep on deck. Only two more days and we'll be landing at a place called Dyea.

September 16, 1897 — Dyea

Writing at first light: Roy is off hiring packhorses. Arrived at Dyea late last night. No docks, just mudflats. Our ship anchored way out, then the baggage was loaded onto scows and taken ashore. Got our gear safely to dry land, but some had to wade in to rescue their floating bundles. We've been told it's less than 35 miles to Lake Bennett. Be there in no time. Then we just float down the Yukon to the goldfields.

September 29, 1897 — Canyon City

Two weeks it's taken to get everything just 8 miles! And now comes the really slow part. No packhorses from here on. Too expensive, Roy says. And the path, we're told, gets steeper and rockier. The drill is to drag a load about a mile, stack the bundles beside the trail under a canvas, then go back for another load — it's called making a cache. Roy's worried about thieves, but everyone seems too busy moving their own gear to meddle with ours.

October 27, 1897 — Sheep Camp

Blinding snowstorm since yesterday. We're stuck in our tent, so finally time to write. From here there's a steep climb 4 miles up Long Hill to the Scales, then up the Golden Stairs to the top of Chilkoot Pass. Doing it once wouldn't be so bad but we can only take 50 pounds at a time. Who knows how many times we'll be up and down that hill. Pal has been a big help, hauling and guarding our supplies, but Roy is starting to worry about how much it costs to feed him. I caught Roy counting our money again today. We never dreamed we'd be so long on the trail.

"Come on, boy! Just a few more steps, Pal." Blinded by swirling snow, Tim heaved against the rope and felt the tug of the sled behind him. How many times had he trudged up Long Hill over the past week? Fifteen? Twenty? And still they had bundles waiting below.

Not that he was alone on the hill. Toiling behind him was another stampeder. And behind him another and another, all lugging supplies up this endless slope. Tim plodded on, trying not to suck too much frigid air into his lungs, ignoring the agony in his back and legs.

For weeks, one thought had kept him going. *We'll be there soon. Soon.* But now another thought had joined the first in a frantic loop round his brain — Roy's order: "The minute we break camp, that dog goes."

The first time Roy said it, Tim thought he'd heard wrong — get rid of Pal? But every night for a week now, Roy had been on at him. "You know it's going to take us longer than we thought." "We're going to need every penny just to get there." "I told you not to bring him and now look what it costs to feed him." "Show some sense and sell him."

Sense? What's so sensible about getting rid of the dog that's pulling all this gear up the hill for us? Tim took a deep breath to calm himself, and felt cold air knife into his lungs. But his mind wouldn't let up.

The truth was, Roy had changed since they'd left Seattle. Just a year ago, standing by their parents' grave, Roy had said, "It's you and me now, buddy. I'll look after you." But that had been before Roy had invested everything in Barton's Grocery Emporium and lost it all. Before he'd spent months walking the streets, looking for work. Now that there was a chance for some real money, he'd become a stranger — a stranger with burning eyes and a restless impatience to get over the mountain, get to the goldfields, get to the gold.

Tim shook his head. Forget it. Just put one foot after the other, he told himself. Get the job done.

Finally the ground leveled out and he no longer had to strain so hard. Pal surged ahead, anxious to reach their cache and get rid of the chafing harness, and Tim had to do a quick side step to keep the sled from running up his heels. He reached out and patted Pal to quiet him, then peered around.

On all sides he could see dimly through the thickly falling snow, shadowy shapes stacking the food and equipment they'd carried from the foot of the mountain up to this halfway mark called the Scales. But where was his own cache? Finally he spotted the marker pole sticking out of a snow-covered mound, topped by one of the garishly striped socks Aunt

Rachel had knit from odds and ends of yarn.

Tim crouched down to hug Pal and borrow some warmth for himself. The sweat he'd worked up climbing Long Hill was turning clammy under the layers of sweaters and his heavy blue mackinaw coat.

They'd had no idea what they were letting themselves in for all those weeks ago in Dyea. Twenty miles and you're over the mountain, a man had assured them. What he didn't say was that the trail ran through scrub forests littered with fallen trees, zigged and zagged across the river, wound through a boulder-strewn canyon and then abruptly headed straight up a mountain, where it ran for ages along the edge of a sheer drop. Nor had anyone warned them how soon and how swiftly winter would set in. They'd been weeks getting their stuff over the first few miles. And tomorrow they faced the Golden Stairs, the last, worst 1000 feet of all.

"And that's another thing," Roy had said one night over a meal of

beans and bread. He set down his fork and looked Tim in the eye. "I've climbed those Stairs. They're killers. There's no way you'll get Pal up there. The kindest thing would be to sell him to Flannigan over at the store. He'd be better off there."

For a moment Roy had sounded like his old self — like the big brother who's always looked out for him. Tim felt himself wavering. Maybe Roy was right. What if he *couldn't* get Pal up the Stairs? Pal whined softly and Tim's heart flipped. I can't leave him. I'll find a way. I have to.

But how? That was the question. Tim stacked the last of their bundles on top of their cache, then headed toward the start of the slope some joker had called the Golden Stairs. Fifteen hundred steps cut into sheer ice up a thirty-five degree slope. And somewhere, among the antlike line of climbers slipping, sliding and staggering to the top, was Roy, backpacking another fifty pounds of provisions to the summit.

"She's some steep, all right," wheezed a voice at his shoulder. Tim turned. The man looked like countless others on the trail, a shapeless bundle of woolen coat and hat, ear lugs pulled well down. His face was a wild frizz of eyebrows and beard, all frosted with ice crystals. But from the center of this hairy mass twinkled bright blue eyes. "Just look at them crazy galoots staggerin' up there. The stuff they brought! Nobody needs half that. You sure won't catch Ned Mumby breakin' his back that way." He spat a great stain of brown tobacco juice onto the white snow. "Seen a piano go up just two days ago."

"A piano? Up there?"

"Yep. Piece by piece. On the backs of three of them packers. Cost a fortune, I reckon. Some people got more money than sense."

"On their backs?"

Ned Mumby nodded. "Most everything gets to the top, gets there on somebody's back. No other way." A raspy chuckle left three puffs of white vapor hanging in the cold air. "Well, I'll be shovin' off now. See you at the top."

Tim stared into the distance, one mitt rubbing his tingling nose. On someone's back. "You hear that, Pal? That's how we'll do it. That's exactly how we'll do it."

As he trudged the next two loads up Long Hill, Tim made a plan. A canvas sack and some boards for stiffening. He'd seen just what he needed abandoned along the trail. Thank goodness he'd been training Pal to obey. Never seen a dog so smart. Learned to heel in one day — and he'd sit still as a statue for hours. Reckon there's some bird dog in him somewhere, Aunt Rachel had said.

By that evening, when Roy came plodding back to their tent, Tim had hidden away a good length of rope and a sturdy sack just the right size.

"Time to strike camp," Roy said, and Tim's chest tightened. "We'll pack the rest of this stuff onto the sled in the morning. If the weather holds, you can climb the Stairs tomorrow." He glanced at Pal, who lay across Tim's feet, tail thumping. "And remember what I said, Tim. First thing tomorrow take Pal over to Flannigan's."

Next morning, Tim watched with relief as Roy tramped off. It took until noon to get the last two loads up Long Hill, but finally Tim was ready to tackle the dreaded Golden Stairs. He was frantic to get on with it — Roy might come tobogganing down the slope any minute, the way all the stampeders did once they'd dropped their loads at the summit. He shook out the canvas sack, threaded the rope through loops at the sides and fitted a square of wood into the bottom for Pal to sit on. "Come on, boy. In you go. Now sit. Sit!"

Pal was quite willing to sit on the square of wood, but he began to whimper and shift when Tim drew the sack up. "It's all right, boy. I won't cover your face."

He had knotted the rope into a rough halter and was trying to figure out how to heave the sack onto his back when a wheezy voice said, "Well, if that don't beat all."

It was Ned Mumby, stowing another load on his cache. "Your canine friend doesn't look too happy. You reckon to drag him up those stairs in that contraption?"

"Not drag," Tim protested. "I'm going to carry him to the top, on my back. I'm going to use this rope for straps and . . ." His voice trailed away. It had all seemed quite possible last night.

"Reckon you could learn a thing or two from them piano movers, son. Thing is, they work in pairs — like a team. Here, you stand steady and I'll sling the whole shebang up."

15

Ned gripped the canvas sack and hoisted. "Now slide those ropes over your shoulders. That's it. Cross the ends over your chest and I'll tie the rest around you and the sack."

Tim leaned forward to ease the pull on his shoulders as Ned made tight knots in the rope. "That's the idea. Your friend there won't be happy if he feels himself slipping."

Pal had been making unhappy yipping sounds throughout the whole procedure. "It's okay, boy. It's okay." Tim could feel Pal's heartbeats thudding right through the sack and his own thick coat, but the whimpering stopped.

"Here, take this staff. You'll need it on them stairs."

"I can't take your staff," Tim protested. He knew from the scavenging he and Roy had done to build fires just how scarce wood was.

"Don't you worry. I always carry a spare. Now, off you go, son, before that dog of yours takes it into his mind to jump out."

"Sit, boy." Tim made his voice stern, and the bundle on his back stopped shifting. "Good boy. Good boy." As he soothed Pal, Tim edged into the line of men, each bent under his own awkward load.

The "Stairs" were little more than toeholds punched into the ice, with a rope strung alongside as a marker. Tim took a deep breath. This is it, then. He dug the staff into the snow, set the toe of one leather boot into the first slippery cut and started up. As he moved from the safety of one step to the uncertainty of the next, the pack shifted slightly. Pal whimpered. Tim heard someone mutter, "Crazy kid," and it set Aunt Rachel's words drumming through his head. "You're crazy to think you'll strike it rich. Crazy, crazy, crazy!" The beat of the words pushed him forward.

Step and heave, step and heave. Minute after minute, or had it been hour after hour? How much longer? If he straightened even slightly, he could feel the bundle pull backward and Pal shift uneasily. Keep still, boy. Please keep still. Pain was shooting down his neck and along his shoulders. He didn't dare look up. The load might shift.

Above him and to the side, Tim could see one of the resting places Roy had mentioned. A few men sat on benches hacked out of the snow and ice. Tim heaved himself up another step. Did he dare take a break? A sudden gust of snow blinded him. He instinctively put up one hand to clear his eyes.

"You! Watch it there!" came an angry voice from behind.

Jamming the staff into snow to steady himself, Tim pushed up again, back into the rhythm of the line. Aunt Rachel's "Crazy, crazy, crazy" thrummed through him as he followed the feet above, dodged the hands that clawed below. One more step. One more step.

And suddenly he could see over the top. Fingers aching from the cold, Tim braced himself against an icy ledge and felt for the next step. His boot found a level spot. He straightened his leg and the heave pushed him over the top. A short scramble on hands and knees and he was on level ground. Pal, wiggling out of the sack, knocked him flat, but in a second Tim had rolled over and was on his knees, hugging his exuberant companion.

"Keep movin', boy." A gruff voice came from behind, urging Tim up the slippery pathway, away from the edge. But there was something he had to do first. Clutching Pal's collar he turned to look back. Through the swirling snow he could barely see the long, long sweep down the valley they had been climbing for so many weeks.

"You're crazy!" Aunt Rachel's words again. And for the first time since he'd left Seattle, Tim wondered if just maybe she'd been right.

THE STAMPEDE

"Gold! Gold! GOLD!" Newsboys all across North America stood on street corners shouting the incredible news. It had sped down the telegraph wires from San Francisco, where the steamship SS *Excelsior* had docked on July 15, 1897, full of Klondike gold. Even more gold would be arriving on a second ship. A crowd of 5000 was waiting impatiently that July 17 in 1897 as the SS *Portland* steamed into Seattle.

When the gangplank was lowered, down it came scruffy men in threadbare clothes dragging trunks, wooden cases, even bedrolls stuffed to bursting with gold dust and nuggets. Some containers were so heavy that two people working together couldn't lift them. Onlookers marveled and asked one another, "They're from where? Alaska?"

"Beyond Alaska," others said. "They've come from the Klondike!"

The Klondike, a place so remote most people had never heard the name before, was suddenly the one spot in the world everyone was talking about. Gold had been discovered there — lying about in creek beds, so rumor said. A person could become rich just by bending down and scooping it up.

People who one minute were trimming hair, driving carts or baking bread abandoned jobs, homes and families in the mad dash to the goldfields. This great rush of people, like a herd of cattle running out of control, was called a stampede. Years later, people who had made the trek north to the Klondike were proud to be known as stampeders.

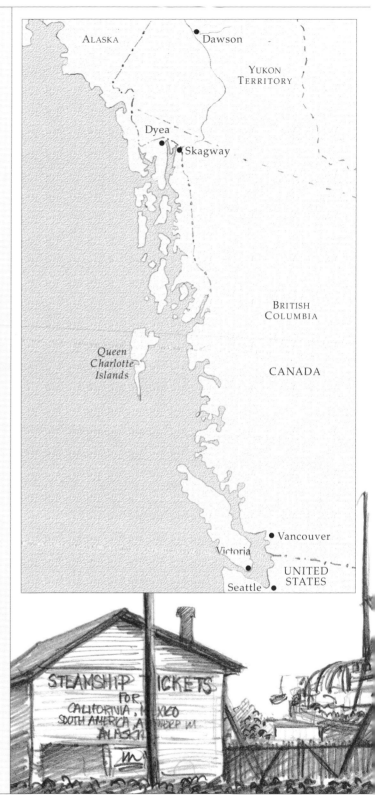

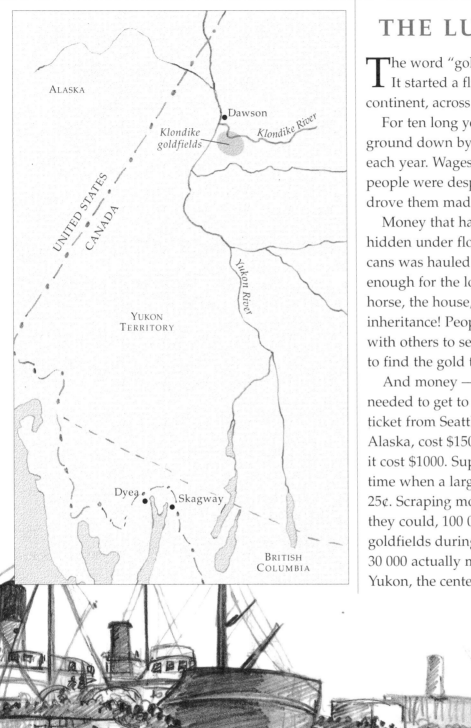

ALASKA

Dawson

Klondike goldfields

Klondike River

UNITED STATES

CANADA

Yukon River

YUKON TERRITORY

Dyea

Skagway

BRITISH COLUMBIA

THE LURE OF GOLD

The word "gold" was like a match to tinder. It started a flash fire roaring across the continent, across the world.

For ten long years, North America had been ground down by a depression that worsened each year. Wages were low, jobs were scarce, people were desperate. The news of gold drove them mad.

Money that had been hoarded in mattresses, hidden under floorboards or stashed in tin cans was hauled out and counted. Was it enough for the long trek? Then let's sell the horse, the house, the business. Let's use the inheritance! People even pooled their money with others to send one strong young man off to find the gold that would make them all rich.

And money — lots of it — was certainly needed to get to the goldfields. A steamer ticket from Seattle, Washington, to Dyea, Alaska, cost $150 in July 1897. Six months later it cost $1000. Supplies for a year cost $600, at a time when a large meal could be bought for 25¢. Scraping money together whatever way they could, 100 000 people started out for the goldfields during the years 1897 and 1898 — 30 000 actually made it all the way to Dawson, Yukon, the center of the gold rush.

THE GRUBSTAKE

Oldtimers called the money they needed to buy a year's supply of food their grubstake. The valleys of the Yukon River may have been teeming with gold, but there was precious little for a person to eat while he gathered it. Every single item needed to keep a person alive and comfortable for a year had to be carried in by backpack, sled or riverboat. The North-West Mounted Police turned back any stampeder who lacked the food or cash to

Provisions were packed in 23 kg (50 lb.) bundles, sewn into canvas sacks and then wrapped in oilskin to keep them dry. Roy and Tim's list looked like this:

FOOD

400 lb. flour
50 lb. cornmeal
50 lb. oatmeal
35 lb. rice
100 lb. beans
40 lb. candles
100 lb. sugar
8 lb. baking powder
200 lb. bacon
2 lb. soda
36 yeast cakes
15 lb. salt
1 lb. pepper
1/2 lb. mustard
1/4 lb. ginger
25 lb. evaporated apples
25 lb. evaporated peaches
25 lb. evaporated apricots
25 lb. evaporated onions
25 lb. evaporated potatoes
25 lb. dried fish
10 lb. pitted plums
24 lb. coffee
5 lb. tea
4 doz. tins condensed milk
5 bars laundry soap
60 boxes matches
15 lb. soup vegetables
25 cans butter

EQUIPMENT

4 blankets
4 towels,
5 yd. mosquito netting
sleeping bag
Yukon stove
3 granite buckets
cup
plate
knife
fork
2 spoons
2 frying pans
coffee pot
canvas tent

MINING EQUIPMENT

gold pan
pick
2 shovels
handsaw
whipsaw
whetstone
hatchet
3 files
drawknife
ax
3 chisels
20 lb. nails
butcher knife
hammer
compass
jack plane
square
200 ft. rope
15 lb. pitch
10 lb. oakum
Yukon sled

support themselves for a year. Word got around that a tonne (ton) of goods was needed.

Tim and Roy tore a list of necessities from the newspaper. The stores in Seattle were only too happy to supply them with everything they needed. All along the Pacific coast, in cities such as San Francisco, Seattle, Victoria and Vancouver, store owners were mining their own gold from the eager stampeders.

WINTER CLOTHING

SUMMER CLOTHING

hood over a hat with earflaps

a coat made from heavy wool cloth called mackinaw

canvas mittens stuffed with hay or grass for warmth

mackinaw trousers
lace-up boots

broad-brimmed hat with a mosquito-netting veil

overshirt

overalls

For bad weather, a stampeder would also have a heavy rubber-lined coat and an oilskin suit.

snag-proof rubber boots for wading in streams

GETTING TO THE GOLDFIELDS

As they steamed up the coast of British Columbia, the hopeful gold seekers saw a wall of mountains blocking their path to the goldfields. The Coast Mountains were a formidable barrier, with only four places to cross. Most stampeders headed for Chilkoot Pass or White Pass.

They disembarked at one of two small ports in Alaska — Dyea for Chilkoot Pass or Skagway for White Pass. There, they loaded their supplies onto packhorses or their backs and headed toward the mountains.

At first glance, the lower, wider White Pass seemed an easier route. But before winter's cold hardened the trail, it was only a blazed track. Pack animals broke their legs in the tangle of fallen trees or slipped off the narrow ledges to plunge into the river below. Or they sank into the muddy slime of the bog beyond. Soon, the trail was lined with the carcasses of dead horses.

As word of the dangers of White Pass trickled back, most chose Chilkoot Pass. When they docked at Dyea, they were told the mountain pass was less than 32 km (20 mi.) away. Then they discovered that to reach it they would have to pack their provisions over a trail blocked by fallen logs, ford the meandering river several times and struggle through a narrow canyon. This brought them to Sheep Camp, at the foot of Long Hill — and the most difficult part of their journey.

THE CHILKOOT PASS

Sheep Camp was at the base of a mountain. On the other side was a series of lakes and the Yukon River. From there Tim and Roy could travel by boat to Dawson and the goldfields. But to get from one side of the mountain to the other, there was only one way to go — up and over.

Tim and Roy, along with thousands of other stampeders, camped at Sheep Camp and sledded their goods, load by load, 3 km (2 mi.) up Long Hill to the Scales. From there, a set of ice steps called the Golden Stairs rose almost straight up until they reached Chilkoot Pass at the summit — the most difficult climb on the Chilkoot Trail.

Many gave up. The trail was littered with their discarded baggage. Those who made it up the mountain and over Chilkoot Pass were faced with even greater challenges. First they had to sled their equipment down the mountain past Crater Lake to Lake Lindeman or Lake Bennett, and then build boats to transport them the last 965 km (550 mi.) down the Yukon River to the goldfields.

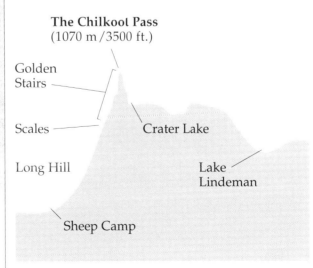

The Chilkoot Pass
(1070 m /3500 ft.)

Golden
Stairs

Scales

Long Hill

Crater Lake

Lake
Lindeman

Sheep Camp

Climbing the Chilkoot

The Golden Stairs, the last 300 m (1000 ft.) of the Chilkoot climb, were cut out of sheer ice. The final 50 m (150 ft.) — about the height of a 12-story building — was almost as straight as a wall. Tim was lucky. He only had to slog up that icy slope once. Roy and the other stampeders had to make the trip at least 40 times to get all their equipment — at 50 pounds a trip — to the summit. Put yourself in the stampeders' boots for a few minutes.

You'll need:
a backpack
a 4.5 kg (10 lb.) bag of potatoes

1. Put the bag of potatoes into the backpack and hoist it onto your back.

2. Start climbing the longest set of stairs you can find. Remember, you can't stop because there's a long line of men climbing right behind you. Also, an icy blizzard is blowing snow in your face. How does your load feel? The stampeders' loads were 5 times as heavy as yours.

3. Now do the math. How many stairs did you climb? The stampeders climbed as many as 1500 stairs cut out of sheer ice. How many sets of stairs would you have to climb to equal that?

4. Climb the stairs again. How long did it take you? The stampeders could go only as quickly as the slowest in line. The climb could take them up to 6 hours.

26

THE PACKERS

The majority of gold seekers carried their tonne (ton) of goods on their own backs. Some, however, could afford to hire professional packers.

The Native people of the area, the Chilkats, had used Chilkoot Pass through the mountains since time immemorial. They had grown up climbing its rock-strewn slopes. They were sturdy and tough. They were also canny businesspeople. As the gold seekers streamed in, Chilkat men, women and children hired themselves out as packers.

The Chilkats could easily carry 45 kg (100 lb.) at a time, twice what most stampeders could manage. As more stampeders arrived, the packers increased their rates from 14¢ per 0.5 kg (1 lb.) to 40¢. And no matter what the agreed-upon rate, the price always went up just before the steepest ascent. At the foot of the Golden Stairs was a flat section called the Scales. Here the packers had set up a large scale where they reweighed every bundle. Because of the steep climb ahead, they increased the price to $1 per 0.5 kg (1 lb.).

Opportunities to make money always attract entrepreneurs. If gold seekers were determined to get their provisions over Chilkoot Pass, how could a clever businessman make it easier? By early 1898, several groups were operating aerial tramways. Horse power or steam power turned wheels that carried large buckets on cables to the top. Each bucket could take 45 kg (100 lb.) of goods. After a few trips up the icy stairs, many stampeders were tempted to spend some of their precious money getting their belongings over the mountain the easy way.

THE CHRONICLERS

Not everyone heading for the Klondike was interested in gold. Some simply wanted an adventure, the adventure of a lifetime. Others wanted to record the adventure. And so, along with the stampeders went journalists and photographers determined to use words or images to bring the adventure to the folks back home.

ERIC A. HEGG, PHOTOGRAPHER

Eric Hegg was 29 when news of the Yukon gold strike broke. He was tired of working in a studio photographing families in their best outfits. He was ready for a bigger adventure. Just getting his equipment to the goldfields was to prove an adventure in itself.

Photography equipment in 1897 was heavy and awkward to transport. The camera was a large wooden box that sat on a tripod. Although film was available, most photographers preferred fragile glass plates. And they also needed chemicals to take and develop the photographs.

Despite the difficulties, by early fall 1897, Hegg and two partners had made it to Dyea. Hegg set up headquarters in a shack built from scows (boats) that had smashed on the beach. From this base he began photographing the struggles of stampeders to haul their supplies off ships, over the tidal flats and over the mountains.

Somewhere he managed to find six goats. When the snow arrived, he hitched them to a sled to carry his photographic equipment and darkroom back and forth along the mountain trail. Hegg and his goats became a familiar sight to men slogging their equipment, load by weary load, up the mountain.

While Hegg earned money selling stampeders pictures of themselves, his two partners were at Lake Bennett building a barge. By May 29, 1898, with a darkroom in place on board, they were ready to join the race downriver to the Yukon. Unlike other stampeders, their goal was not to get to Dawson quickly, but to record the details of the journey. At difficult spots, such as rapids, they beached their boat for several days while Hegg took pictures.

By July they were in Dawson. Hegg set up a studio in a cabin with log walls and a tent roof, then turned his camera on the thousands of

gold seekers crowding the town and the surrounding countryside. He caught dance-hall girls in daring tights, laundresses bent over tubs, miners in high boots leading packhorses as they headed out to their claims, gamblers dressed in broadcloth coats with diamond stickpins in their ties — all tramping through deep, gluey mud just to cross the street. Then he went out to the claims to record the hard labor and heartbreak of extracting gold from frozen muck.

During the three years Hegg spent in Dawson, he went "outside" several times. In 1899 he created a traffic jam in New York when people flocked to his show, eager to see for themselves the incredible feats of bravery and foolishness that mere words in a newspaper article could hardly begin to convey.

Many photographers recorded the gold rush, but it was Eric Hegg who took the picture that for most people summed up the incredible determination of those who made it to the goldfields. His most famous picture shows hundreds of stampeders, each with a stave in one hand, the other hand clutching a guide rope, toiling up the Golden Stairs, packs on their backs, like a line of black ants against the snow-covered mountainside.

This was one of E.A. Hegg's many photographs, of stampeders climbing the Golden Stairs.

FAITH FENTON, JOURNALIST

Faith Fenton was an enterprising spirit whose real name was Alice Freeman. As a schoolteacher in prim and proper Toronto, she had to hide the fact that she was also a crusading journalist.

Under the pen name Faith Fenton, she reported on the treatment of sick or abandoned children and exposed the harsh treatment suffered by the poor. In the late 19th century, these were considered shocking topics for a woman to write about.

The minute Faith heard the word "gold," she realized she had struck the story of the century. That it was taking place in the most remote corner of Canada made the story even more compelling. By spring 1898, she had found a way to get there. A new organization, the Victorian Order of Nurses, was sending four nurses to open a hospital in Dawson. They were to travel with the Yukon Field Force, a unit of 200 soldiers sent to establish a Canadian presence among the thousands of American miners. Faith would travel with the group and send stories to *The Globe*, a Toronto newspaper.

On May 6, 1898, the group left Ottawa by train for Vancouver. They took a steamer up the coast, then an inland route that was supposed to be shorter than White Pass or Chilkoot Pass. After a boat trip up the Stikine River, the men and women faced a hike of 240 km (150 mi.) through mosquito-infested forest and muskeg before reaching the river system that would link them to the Yukon River.

Getting there was more than half the story. Faith's reports to *The Globe* described the incredible difficulty of traveling through fire-devastated wilderness. "Our way lay for interminable miles through dull, smoking trees and over logs yet licked by little flame tongues. We ate our evening meal standing . . . Our tents were pitched upon the sooty ground."

True to her crusading spirit, Faith reported on cruelty to animals, especially the packhorses — "pitiful, weary creatures with great angry blotches like inflamed scalds upon their backs, the result of incompetent packing. The animal walks on in dumb agony, with festering sores goaded every moment by the load above it, until he drops on the trail and is mercifully shot."

Despite the hardships she catalogued, by the end of the three-month journey, Faith was writing, "Come up to the Yukon, O artist of our country! Let our people know the rare summer beauties of this much-maligned land — our beautiful northern Canada."

All too soon, the "rare summer beauties" gave way to harsh winter and Faith found herself stranded in Dawson. She used her secretarial and journalistic skills to support herself, and by spring she was reluctant to leave the North. Instead she married and settled in Dawson until 1904, when she and her husband, Dr. John Elliot Brown, returned to Toronto.

Faith sent nine dispatches to *The Globe* describing her journey to the Klondike. She was one of many journalists who slogged through difficult country under backbreaking conditions looking not for gold, but for a writer's treasure — the story of the century.

31

BUILDING THE BOAT

February 15, 1898

We've been camped at Lake Lindeman for over a week now. Every day we go back up to the summit of Chilkoot Pass to dig out more of our cache. It's buried under nearly 10 feet of snow. Roy was pretty annoyed when he saw I still had Pal. But then someone tried to ransack our cache and Pal scared him off. After that Roy cooled down some. Besides, we have to sled all this stuff down to Lake Bennett. Now that I've made a good solid harness out of rope and canvas, Pal can outpull Roy and me.

February 27, 1898

Finally! Our last load! Pal was a great help on the flat but we all had trouble on the slopes. The trick, we learned from one man on the trail, is to wind a rope around the runners to use as a brake so the sled can't run away on you. We stopped by the North-West Mounted Police tent to pay the duty on our goods. Roy's mad about having to pay, but I kind of feel bad for the Mounties. The wind never stops whipping the snow into blizzards. You can hardly see their tent for the snowdrifts.

March 10, 1898

Lake Bennett at last — and another tent city! All up the slopes, one tent after another. Hundreds of people building boats, getting ready for spring breakup. That's what we'll be doing soon. I've been keeping an eye out for Ned Mumby but I haven't seen him or any of the people who camped near us at Sheep Camp. Funny thing about this trip — you team up with a group one day and the next day they're gone, so you team up with somebody else. A bit lonely, that. Roy's miserable company these days — he's on at me about getting rid of Pal again. Somewhere he heard that big dogs bring in $300 in Dawson. I don't care what Roy says. I'm never selling Pal. His food can come out of my share — even if I starve.

Three logs down, six to go. Tim trudged up the slope, dodging tree branches that littered the ground. Halfway up he paused to catch his breath and look back at the tent city that sprawled along the edge of Lake Bennett. The lower slopes were stripped of trees now. Tim and Roy, along with all the other latecomers, had had to go higher up for their timber. But at last they had the logs they needed for their boat. Now the challenge was getting them down to the lake through the maze of jutting stumps.

Roy was waiting impatiently by their log pile. He had knotted a rope around the end of a log, leaving two long tails. One of these he tossed to Tim. "Let's go," he barked. "That gang next over just took their last log down."

What is this — a contest? But Tim knew better than to protest. The closer they got to the goldfields, the more frenzied Roy seemed to get. Day by day, he'd become more moody and unpredictable, snapping at Tim for the slightest little thing. For the sake of peace, Tim usually just did as he was told. Now, without a word, he grasped his end of the rope.

They had learned to let the log's weight propel it down the slope while they bounded along behind, steering with the guide ropes. Looked easy, Tim thought ruefully, but on balance, he'd rather be dragging a loaded sled up Long Hill. Still, they'd managed the first three logs.

"Pull that rope tighter," Roy yelled, "or it'll snag."

Hauling back on the guide ropes to keep the front end of the log nose up, the brothers maneuvered precariously around stumps and over slash left by previous boatbuilders.

"Look out! We're coming to the steep part."

The log lurched and Tim dug in his heels to brake its downward surge. Reefing on the rope as the log bucked and swayed, Tim spotted a rock outcrop right in their path.

"Watch out!" he yelled.

Roy responded with a sudden tug that whipped the rope out of Tim's hands. He lunged after it and missed. The log slewed sideways down the slope. With a loud crunch it hit the rock outcrop, split halfway along its length and came to rest wedged between two stumps.

"Smashed to smithereens!" Roy threw down his hat. "Blast it all to perdition. A perfectly good log wrecked." He glared at Tim, gritting his teeth as though biting back words.

Tim didn't need to hear the words out loud. They were written plainly on Roy's face. A half-grown kid — what use are you?

With a snarl, Roy scooped up his hat and bounded down the slope.

* * *

Roy was gone for hours. Tim had rubbed grease on his stinging palms, made a batch of biscuits and heated up beans for their supper. He was scraping cornmeal mush from the frying pan into a bowl for Pal when Roy strode briskly into the circle of firelight. Two men followed him. Without a word to Tim, all three hunkered down on the log they used as a bench and helped themselves to the freshly made biscuits.

Tim crouched beside Pal, who was hungrily gulping down his own food. The men's backs made a wall between him and the fire and he shivered as he strained to hear. What was going on?

From the low growl of conversation, a voice suddenly snarled, "A kid? We're teaming up with a kid?" It was the burlier of the two men.

"You're teaming up with me," Roy said stiffly. "*He's* just along as the cook. Are you in or not?"

The second man, slim even in his bulky winter clothes, put out a hand to calm his peppery companion. "We're in," he said. "Young fella's a good cook, we've just had proof of that, and it doesn't take a stevedore's

arm to drive nails." He stood and turned to where Tim hovered just outside the circle of light. "Put 'er there, son. The name's Jake."

Startled, Tim offered his own hand. "Tim."

"See you've scraped yourself," Jake pointed to Tim's palm. "You want to soak that in warm water." He jerked his head toward the other man. "Now, meet Bill. Reckon we'll all be workmates by tomorrow." But Bill just stuffed the last biscuit into his mouth as though to say, Who needs to explain things to a kid?

And then all three of them were gone, leaving Tim with the remains of supper to clear away. Well, he was used to that. "You cook, I'll cart," Roy had decided early on.

Maybe I've been kidding myself, Tim thought as he collected the tin cups the men had left scattered about. Just the other day, he'd watched two men struggling to drag a saw through a freshly felled log. Even in the biting winter wind, sweat dripped off them as they'd strained to pull the two-handled saw through the green timber. Cutting one board had left them panting for breath. If skidding three measly logs left me exhausted, how could I cut planks? But Roy might at least have asked me . . .

"Bill doesn't seem too friendly," Tim ventured later, straightening out his bedroll in their tent.

"He knows boats, that's the important part." Roy was sitting on his own bedroll pulling off his boots. "And Jake's worked as a carpenter." Keeping his eyes fixed on the boot he'd started to grease, he went ·on, "Thought we might as well pool our grub. Get you to cook for all of us. Save time for work."

Tim swallowed. "Yeah, sure." Guess I'm just the hired help now.

* * *

The four quickly fell into a routine. Tim was "chief cook and bottle washer," as Jake put it, while the men did the heavy work of sawing lumber and roughing out the boat. Between mealtimes, Tim's job was to pile the newly sawn lumber or hold down boards as the others cut them to length. And he finally learned how to drive a nail straight.

"No! Pull that blasted thing out and straighten it!" was all he heard from Bill as nail after nail bent under his energetic hammering.

It was Jake who showed him the trick of it. "Son, the secret is to keep your eye on the nail. Once you get the hang of it, two good swings and she's in." Tim loved the feeling of driving the nail straight and true every time. And he loved the neat-fingered way that Jake went about building the boat.

One evening, several weeks after they'd all started working together, Tim and Pal were strolling along the edge of the lake after supper. As the days gradually lengthened, Tim had begun to think that maybe, just maybe, winter would end and finally they would get on their way to the goldfields. But, no, the ice still stretched smooth and white as far as he could see.

Tim sighed, then whistled Pal back from his hunt after interesting smells. "*You* never grumble, do you, boy?" he said as they climbed the slope to their tent. "Cornmeal mush and a walk every day — that's all it takes to keep you happy. Not like some." Just two days ago at the boat site three over, one partner had taken an ax to the side of his scow because the drying planks left gaping seams as they shrank. Tempers were fraying, for sure. But tonight things were peaceful.

On the hard-packed snow Tim's boots made no sound. Passing Jake's tent, he heard a soft shuffling sound. He glanced through the open flap. Jake was sitting cross-legged on his bedroll sliding three small overturned cups around on a board.

Tim crouched down to get a better look. "That a game you're playing, Jake?"

"Move back a bit, son, so's you don't block the light," Jake murmured, his hands moving so quickly that Tim could hardly follow them.

Tim eased to one side to let in the firelight. "Boy, you sure are good at that."

"Just keeping the fingers limber. This cold — a man's hands could stiffen right up. Here," he said, turning over one hand. In his palm was a dried pea. "Show you how it works." He put the pea under one cup, then wove the cups in and around one another. "Where's the pea?"

Tim looked at Jake. "Under that one," he guessed, pointing. Jake lifted the cup. No pea.

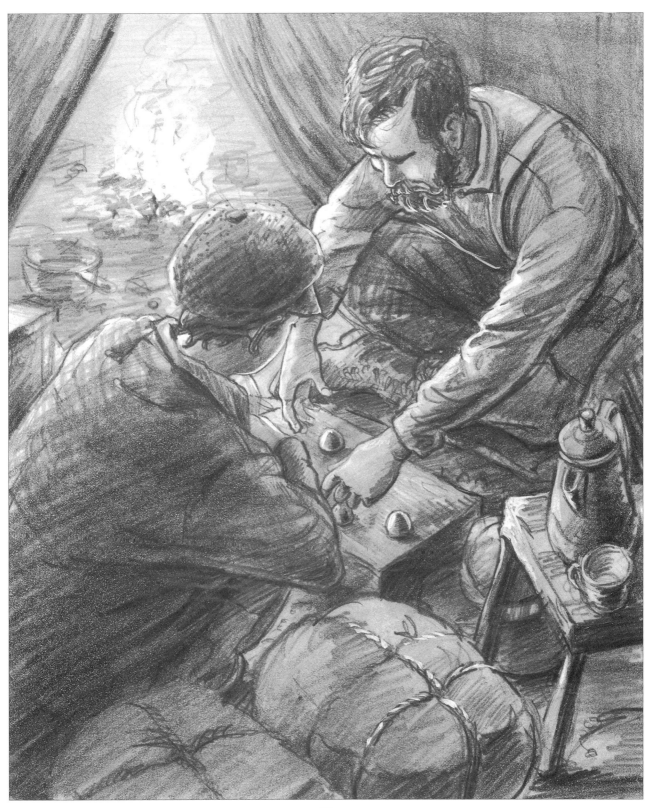

"Try again." This time, as Jake wove the three cups around the board, Tim kept his eyes glued to the one with the pea. Jake's hands stopped and Tim pointed. Jake lifted the cup and — sure enough — there was the pea.

"Good eye you've got." Jake's warm tone made Tim glow.

"Are you a magician, Jake?"

"I've done a few tricks in my time. Tell you what, though. I'm not keen to spread the word. Wouldn't want the others to think I'm slacking off. Be obliged if you'd keep it under your hat."

Tim was about to nod when Jake said, "Well, look at that! See you've got something else under your hat." With a flourish of his hand he produced a coin seemingly from Tim's ear.

"Mum's the word, eh?" Jake said, dropping the coin into Tim's hand.

Jake began packing the cups carefully into a tiny box. Tim looked at the coin, then back at Jake, a prickle of unease spoiling the enchantment.

After that, Tim took to watching Jake out of the corner of his eye as they worked on the boat. The precise way Jake fitted together the decking on their scow, making seams so tight they hardly needed caulking, was impressive, but there were other good carpenters around. No, the odd thing about Jake came with the evenings. While Roy and Bill hunched exhausted near the fire with mugs of tea, Jake would fetch a black broad-brimmed hat from his tent and disappear for hours.

One evening, as Tim stood alone by the fire stirring beans and bacon in the frying pan, a distant shouting startled him. Suddenly Jake was there, stuffing his broad-brimmed hat behind the woodpile and pulling on a flat cap of Roy's.

"Need a bit of help, son," he whispered, casting a quick glance over his shoulder. The shouting came closer.

Tim hesitated for a second, then shoved a tin plate into Jake's hands.

Jake hunched down on the log and Tim spooned beans onto the plate, noting that it shook slightly in Jake's hands. He put the frying pan back over the fire and turned toward two red-faced men who came panting up.

"Feller in a big black hat come past here?"

"Ah — yup," Tim said slowly. "Went that way." He waved with his spoon up the hill, blocking their view of the campsite with his body until they had blundered off between two rows of tents.

Jake put his plate down. "Thanks, Tim." He slid one hand inside his jacket and Tim caught a glimpse of banknotes.

Don't! he thought. The look on Tim's face must have warned Jake. The hand came out empty. "Thanks," Jake said again. "I'm beholden."

Tim stared at Jake. Tell me what's going on. But Jake just turned to scrape his plate into the fire.

I lied for you, Tim thought. You could at least — A noise distracted him. It was Roy, followed by a stranger. Tim's heart gave a thud. That bulky fur parka meant North-West Mounted Police.

"Constable West here seems to think you can help him," Roy said to Jake.

"I'm looking for a man about your build, sir, wearing a broad-brimmed black hat. I have information he's been running a thimblerig game."

Jake ostentatiously pushed back Roy's checkered cap and scratched his head. "Afraid I can't help you."

"Just the same, you'll not object if I have a look around your tent."

"Help yourself." Jake tipped the dregs of his tea into the fire, his back to Roy.

Tim hunkered down by the fire, his arms around Pal as the constable searched. Jake was pouring himself another cup of tea. How could he be so calm when he knew what the constable was about to find?

The Mountie was back, hard-faced but empty-handed. "Just to let you know — we've got some pretty angry men out there who've been bilked of their bankroll. No doubt you're all aware that we have orders to confiscate any gambling equipment we find?"

Roy nodded. Jake just stared into the fire.

"We'll be keeping a sharp eye on any likely suspects. Anybody we catch cheating miners will be escorted to the American border. I'd be obliged if you'd pass the word."

Roy nodded again. As the constable marched off, Tim saw Roy staring at the cap Jake was still wearing, and his stomach knotted. Roy's temper was on a hairtrigger these days. But to Tim's amazement, Roy said nothing, just stamped off into the dark night.

When he had gone Jake sidled around to the back of Roy and Tim's tent. He returned with a folded-up tripod, a tray and a familiar small box. Tim felt sick. So that's the thanks I get. Uses my tent and doesn't even care if I know — now that I've lied for him.

Jake said nothing. Once he'd tucked the tripod into his own tent and tossed Roy's cap onto its usual peg he, too, slipped off out of the firelight.

"I thought Jake was a friend," Tim wrote by the light of the dying fire, "but it turns out he's a crook . . ." He heard steps and quickly shut the journal. It was Roy.

"Where's Jake?"

"Couldn't say." Tim kept his eyes on his journal.

There was a long silence. He looked up to see Roy frowning at him. Then Roy's eyes widened. He reached behind the woodpile and picked up Jake's broad-brimmed hat. "You covered for him, didn't you? And gave him my cap to put that Mountie off the track."

Roy grabbed Tim's arm and the journal went flying. Pal sprang up snarling and Tim, more frightened for Pal than for himself, said, "Quiet, boy."

"You know what Jake does, don't you?"

Tim pulled his arm out of Roy's grasp. "Sort of."

"Sort of! He's a four-flushing cheat. He fleeced those numskulls. That's why they were after him."

"I played that game with him. Picked the right cup just like that. Nothing to it."

"Grow up. He *let* you win. You think he plays fair when money's involved?"

After that, the atmosphere was tense. Bill, always gruff, had never added much to the conversation. Now Roy said only what was necessary. And even though Jake seemed as calm as ever, Tim noticed that he and his broad-brimmed hat never disappeared after supper. Despite the strain, the boat took shape until finally there was nothing left to do but tap caulking into the seams and waterproof it with tar.

One morning when they'd almost finished the caulking, Tim woke to the sound of a loud shout. What was happening? He scrambled out of

his bedroll and grabbed his trousers. Roy just groaned and rolled over. By the time Tim was outside, the whole camp was on the move. Men were doing up buttons as they ran. Some still in long johns hopped barefoot through the last of the snow. Women clutched shawls around their shoulders. Everyone ran pell-mell toward the lake.

"It's the ice!" someone in front shouted. "She's breakin'up. We're on our way, boys!"

Tim paused just long enough to untie Pal's lead, then they were off, pushing through the crowd to reach the shore. And sure enough the surface of the lake was a crazy quilt of jostling white shapes surrounded by ever-widening black lines. They'd finished the scow just in time.

When Tim and Pal returned to the campsite, Roy and Jake were sitting calmly around the fire pit watching bacon sputter in the frying pan.

"No need to get het up," Jake said. "It'll be the better part of two days before the ice clears. Take us that long to load the scow."

Everywhere in camp the mood had changed. The smell of melting tar rose on all sides as boatbuilders hurried to finish waterproofing the seams of their boats. Everyone was feeling lighthearted at the thought of finally getting on with the journey. Roy didn't even scowl when Tim fed Pal the last of his biscuits.

"Time to see how she floats," was all he said. "Then we can load her up."

It was all a blur after that — sliding the scow down to the water, cheering when she actually floated and stayed afloat after several hours of the planks "taking up" water and, finally, hauling their goods on board.

Tim and Roy had planned the loading carefully — spare clothing and mining equipment on the bottom, wrapped in plenty of oilcloth to keep them dry, food packs and cooking equipment close at hand on top.

Now they were almost ready. As Roy and Bill struggled with the stiff tarpaulin that was to be their sail, Tim lashed down the cargo.

He had just finished tying down the last of the bundles when Jake came aboard carrying something with long handles wrapped in oilcloth. Tim felt a flash of annoyance. Mining gear should have been stowed on the bottom of the load.

"That your pick and shovel?"

Bill let out a hoot of laughter. "What would old Jake want with *mining* gear?" he scoffed.

"Keep ahold of that end, will you?" Roy shouted and Bill went back to wrestling with the sail.

As Jake placed the bundle high on the load, out of harm's way, Tim realized what it was — the thimblerig outfit. "Thought you'd given that up."

Jake shrugged. "So I gamble a bit, son — no harm done. Life's one big gamble."

"Roy says you rig the game. Life's not like that."

"No? Aren't we all gambling on our chances of getting down the river? If I'm a good sailor and you're not, isn't the game rigged in my favor?"

The scow gave a lurch and Tim sat down hard on the pile of cooking pots he'd just lashed in place. Jake sounded so reasonable, and yet . . . he cheated people. But he treated me right, Tim told himself, remembering the lessons in boatbuilding, the kind words for meals cooked. He isn't all bad.

"Grab a pole," Roy shouted and Tim jumped up to help push off. The crowd on shore cheered as the wind caught and filled the sail.

"We're off!" Tim felt his spirits lift with the breeze. He pulled his pole out of the water and turned to find himself staring at Jake's bundled-up thimblerig outfit. Forget Jake for now, he decided. We're on our way at last. That's all that matters.

BOATBUILDING

Getting over the mountains was just the first hurdle on the way to Dawson and the goldfields. Ahead of the stampeders stretched 1000 km (600 mi.) of heavily forested wilderness. A few kept right on, sledding their provisions down from the passes and then over the frozen lakes and rivers. But most camped beside Lake Lindeman or Lake Bennett until the ice broke up. They spent their time building rafts, scows, barges — anything that would float their goods north to the goldfields.

Boatbuilding was not a one-person job, so stampeders looked around the crowded tent city for partners. The ideal team comprised a carpenter, a cook and an experienced sailor — all with good, strong backs. As they worked, North-West Mounted Police (NWMP) constables made their rounds and advised first-time boat-builders. "Make your boats long and strong. The Yukon is both. Don't start out in a floating coffin."

On May 30, 1898, with the ice slowly clearing out of Lake Bennett, every type of craft imaginable set sail for gold country. The NWMP kept lists of all the boats. As a result, they knew that exactly 7124 boats would be traveling through the treacherous rapids and mosquito-infested calms of the Yukon River on the way to Dawson.

Cutting the Trees
Boatbuilding teams hiked 3 km (2 mi.) up the mountain valley to find five or six spruce or pine trees. They carried the logs, one by one, on their shoulders or used ropes to help skid them down the mountain.

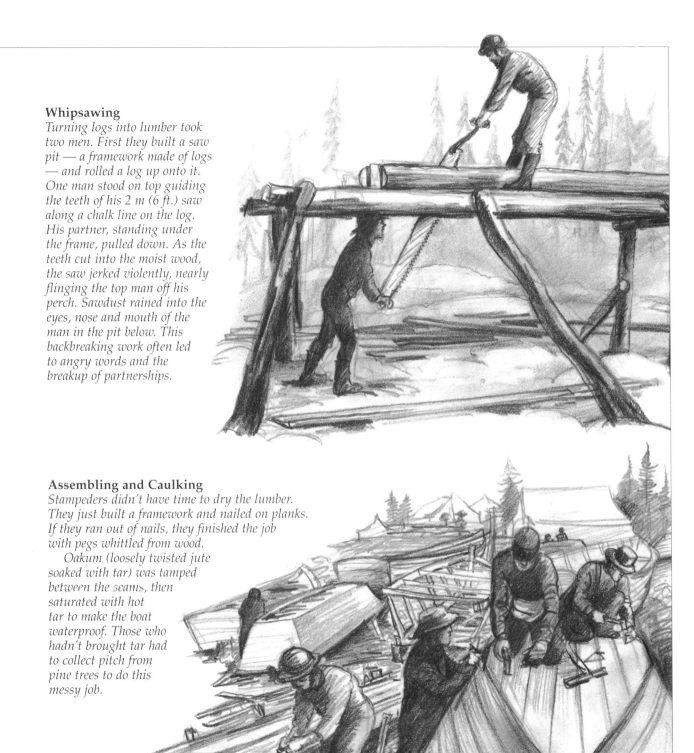

Whipsawing

Turning logs into lumber took two men. First they built a saw pit — a framework made of logs — and rolled a log up onto it. One man stood on top guiding the teeth of his 2 m (6 ft.) saw along a chalk line on the log. His partner, standing under the frame, pulled down. As the teeth cut into the moist wood, the saw jerked violently, nearly flinging the top man off his perch. Sawdust rained into the eyes, nose and mouth of the man in the pit below. This backbreaking work often led to angry words and the breakup of partnerships.

Assembling and Caulking

Stampeders didn't have time to dry the lumber. They just built a framework and nailed on planks. If they ran out of nails, they finished the job with pegs whittled from wood.

Oakum (loosely twisted jute soaked with tar) was tamped between the seams, then saturated with hot tar to make the boat waterproof. Those who hadn't brought tar had to collect pitch from pine trees to do this messy job.

STEELE OF THE MOUNTED

Samuel B. Steele, Superintendent of the North-West Mounted Police for the Yukon

The man attracting all the attention was Samuel B. Steele, Superintendent of the North-West Mounted Police for the Yukon. In 1866, at 17, Sam Steele joined the Canadian militia. In 1870 he was part of the Red River Expedition sent to restore order in the territory soon to become Manitoba. When the North-West Mounted Police was formed in 1873 to bring order to the west, Steele joined up. With his gift for policing and lawmaking, he rose quickly in the ranks. In 1898 the small NWMP outpost in the Yukon was faced with thousands of miners flocking in from all parts of the world. Sam Steele, with his years of frontier experience, was put in charge.

At Lakes Lindeman and Bennett, Steele watched the stampeders frantically build boats and worried about the confusion that spring breakup would bring. He sent his men out to number every boat and list every occupant's name and address so that records could be kept at checkpoints along the route.

On May 29, when the ice broke up, Steele set out in a small steamer for the first trouble spot, Miles Canyon. Of the boats that went through before he arrived, 150 were smashed and five people drowned. Steele immediately stopped the flood of boats and issued orders:

Fragile crafts were to be turned back, amateur sailors could not proceed until they had hired a competent helmsman from lists kept by the NWMP, and women and children must walk the 8 km (5 mi.) around the rapids. The fine for disobeying was $100. Some stampeders resented Steele's orders, but his foresight minimized further deaths. Thousands traveled down the river that June. Although some boats foundered on the rocks, few people drowned. To the families of the unfortunates, Superintendent Steele personally wrote sympathy letters and oversaw the return of their belongings.

Sam Steele's character was as full of steel as his name. He was driven by a sense of duty to his country and to his position. So feared and respected did he make the Mounties in the North that people claimed a miner could leave a trunk full of gold on the main street of Dawson and find it there when he returned.

In 1899 Sam Steele left the North to join the regular army and to train troops, first in the South African War and later in World War I. When he died in 1919, his services had been honored by a knighthood from King George V, but his two short years in the Yukon earned him his most impressive title — the Lion of the North.

THE NORTH-WEST MOUNTED POLICE

Stampeders who reached the tops of White and Chilkoot Passes were startled to find the trail barred by the North-West Mounted Police, who refused to let them pass unless they could prove they had a year's worth of supplies.

The North-West Mounted Police, or Mounties as they were called, was an organization with 20 years of experience policing frontier lands. Its men had set up forts across the West, cleaned up the liquor trade, acted as magistrates to settle disputes and established good relations with Native peoples. It had earned a well-deserved reputation for honesty and fairness.

Policing the Yukon should have been more of the same, but by 1897 the Mounties found themselves facing a formidable challenge. Suddenly they had to cope with the influx of thousands of people, many of whom had no experience surviving in a northern climate. They also had to guard the border against the criminals and con men who came to strike it rich in their own way.

The mountain passes were the only way into Canada, so the North-West Mounted Police set up their border checks at the tops of White and Chilkoot Passes. By doing this, they firmly established the border between Canada and the United States.

At these border posts, stampeders found customshouses, where they had to pay duty on the goods they were carrying, and a new set of rules. All guns had to be licensed, no handguns were allowed, and anyone found with gamblers' marked cards or other gambling equipment was refused entry. Some stampeders were furious. "What if I just shoot my way into Canada?" one demanded. "Start shooting," invited the officer on duty. "That's the quickest way to find out." The man decided to head back to American territory.

Bundled against the raging winds in their thick fur parkas, the Mounties checked more than 22 000 stampeders through the passes the winter of 1897/98. The hordes quickly moved on but the Mounties were stuck, enduring month after month of raging blizzards on an exposed mountaintop. They lived in tents and plank cabins, existing on bad rations and sleeping under roofs that dripped water as the snow melted.

In spring, some moved on to the tent cities along the lakes, then monitored the Yukon River as thousands of stampeders made their way to Dawson. Their calm presence and strict enforcement of the law brought order to what could have been a wild and chaotic frontier.

THE RACE FOR DAWSON

June 2, 1898

Late evening but still full light. Here we sit smack in the middle of Lake Bennett. With the mountains rising on all sides, it's like floating in a soup bowl. So many boats set sail this morning that I can hardly see the water. All day, the whole flotilla was running before the wind. (That's how Bill says it. He's the one who knows all about sailing.) But now the breeze has died and we are all becalmed — the whole kit and caboodle of us. The lake might as well be frozen for all the progress we're making.

Many difficulties were in store for the thousands racing toward Dawson. The worst came at Miles Canyon. Plunging into the gloom between 30 m (100 ft.) high rock walls, the stampeders found themselves suddenly swirling in a whirlpool. The lucky ones spun out, then faced the turbulent waters of Squaw and White Horse Rapids.

On the Yukon River, heading towards Dawson, stampeders faced rapids and whirlpools.

Beyond these rapids, the Yukon River stretched 800 km (500 mi.) north to Dawson. It looked as calm and safe as a summer Sunday outing, but there were hazards for the unwary. Most stampeders slipped easily through Five-Finger Rapids, warned by the Mountie on guard to follow the right-hand channel between tall rock fingers. And the stampeders were now used to ravenous mosquitoes, vicious horseflies and the fierce sun that burned exposed skin. But it took constant vigilance and good eyesight to spot snagged logs that might stave in a boat's side.

Each evening, when they pulled up on shore to make a hot meal, Tim wrapped himself in mosquito netting and recorded the funny, scary and sad sights of the day. Would anyone ever believe these stories when he got back to Seattle?

Sourdough Biscuits

March 15, 1898

Mrs. Carter, in the next tent over, showed me how to make sourdough starter.

She says if I can keep the starter working, we'll always have tasty biscuits.

Instead of yeast breads, stampeders often made sourdough bread and biscuits. They began by making a "sourdough starter." When they made biscuits they would use some of this starter and add flour and water to the remaining starter to keep it going. One batch of starter could last for months or even years. Miners who had spent at least one winter in the Yukon called themselves "sourdoughs." Here is a sourdough starter for biscuits.

You'll need:

375 mL	milk	1 1/2 c.
175 mL	water	3/4 c.
15 mL	sugar	1 tbsp.
5 mL	salt	1 tsp.
0.5 L	flour	2 c.

cheesecloth
string or a large elastic band

1. Combine the milk and water in a pot. Ask an adult to turn on the stove to medium. Heat the mixture until it is warm but not hot.

2. Pour the mixture into a bowl. Stir in the sugar and salt.

3. Add the flour and mix into a smooth paste.

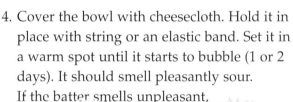

4. Cover the bowl with cheesecloth. Hold it in place with string or an elastic band. Set it in a warm spot until it starts to bubble (1 or 2 days). It should smell pleasantly sour. If the batter smells unpleasant, throw it out and start again.

To make sourdough biscuits, you'll need:

250 mL	sourdough starter	1 c.
1.125 L	all purpose flour	4 1/2 c.
500 mL	warm water	2 c.
5 mL	salt	1 tsp.
5 mL	baking soda	1 tsp.
30 mL	oil (or bacon drippings)	2 tbsp.

1. At least 4 hours before starting the biscuits, pour 250 mL (1 c.) of starter into bowl. Stir into it 625 mL (2 1/2 c.) of the flour and 500 mL (2 c.) of warm water. Cover and set in a warm place.

2. When the starter bubbles, remove 250 mL (1 c.) of it and store it in a glass jar in the refrigerator for future use. That way, like the stampeders, you'll always have sourdough starter when you need it.

3. In a clean bowl mix the remaining 500 mL (2 c.) of flour, the salt and baking soda. Stir in the remaining bubbling starter and mix well.

4. Turn the dough out onto a floured counter and sprinkle a little flour on top. Use a rolling pin to roll the dough out to a thickness of about 1 cm (1/2 in.).

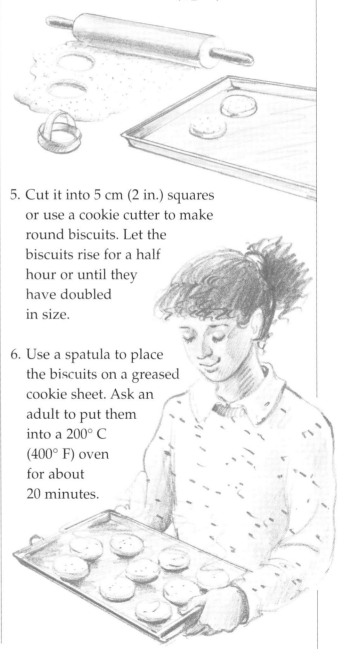

5. Cut it into 5 cm (2 in.) squares or use a cookie cutter to make round biscuits. Let the biscuits rise for a half hour or until they have doubled in size.

6. Use a spatula to place the biscuits on a greased cookie sheet. Ask an adult to put them into a 200° C (400° F) oven for about 20 minutes.

DAWSON

June 16, 1898

Spent all yesterday spreading our gear out to dry after we came a cropper against a snagged log. Bill went right over the side. Served him right after what he did to me at Miles Canyon. We were camped on shore waiting our turn to head into the canyon when a Mountie came by. "Women and children are to walk along the shore," he said and pointed at me. I told him I helped build the boat but he just answered, "Superintendent Steele's orders." Bill laughed like a jackass — and embarrassed me even more. So we walked, Pal and me — but we sure had a good view. Down at the bottom of the canyon, the boats looked like pieces of bark getting tossed around. I could hardly breathe until I saw them pop out of that canyon like a cork out of a bottle.

June 20, 1898

We made it past Split-Up Island but it was a close-run thing. We saw men living on the island, so fed up with each other they refused to travel an inch farther. A Mountie said one pair even sawed their scow in half so neither would have the advantage of the other. I can believe that — Bill and Roy have been at each other for days now. We passed the mouth of the Pelly today. One more river and we'll be at the Klondike.

June 29, 1898

Dawson at last! We knew it was near. There's a hill with a white scar slashed down its face — the Midnight Dome, it's called. You can see it from away back. Finally we heard a great roaring, then we swung around the bend and saw the Klondike River pouring into the Yukon. A great shout went up from all the boats around us. We'd arrived!

June 30, 1898

Well, Dawson is sure nothing to write home about. The river flooded it a month ago and left it like a swamp. All I can see from the docks are log buildings and tents. Jake and Bill took off the minute we touched shore. Roy was glad to be shut of them. So was I, but let's face it — without partners, where will we find the cash to stake a claim? It cost a lot more to get here than we reckoned on. Besides, rumor has it the best claims are already staked.

"How could Roy do this to me?" Tim stomped through wet sand, blind to the crowds buzzing around stalls along Dawson's waterfront. Pal stopped to sniff a pile of rubber boots. Tim gave an angry tug at the lead, then felt guilty. "Not your fault, boy." No, it was Roy's.

Five hours I stood in line to get that miner's license. And what did Roy do? Grabbed the license and lit out for the hills on his own. "One can travel faster than two," he said. "Look out for our gear," he said.

"Are we partners or not?" Tim had flung at Roy's departing back. Much good it had done. Here he was, left behind again.

As the anger dissolved into gloom, Tim found himself bumping into people, pushed along by a crowd eager to scoop up bargains — rubber boots, flannel shirts, shovels, picks. Anything and everything was offered for sale by stampeders anxious for the price of a ticket home. Tim picked up a gold pan. Selling their wrecked dreams, he thought.

Pal tugged at the lead. "What is it, boy?" A delicious smell was making his mouth water. He followed Pal down the line to a sign that shouted "Waffles!"

"Well, will ya look at what the tide washed in."

"Mr. Mumby!" The sight of a friendly face made Tim's spirits soar. "You remember me, do you? Tim? Tim Olsen."

The bright blue eyes twinkled at Tim, then looked down at Pal. "Well, I sure remember this one. Quite the sultan he looked riding up the Golden Stairs in style." Ned Mumby turned to a girl standing behind the stall's makeshift counter. "Tim here toted this big fella up that trail on his back, he did."

Tim's smile was met with a stony stare.

"Meet my friend Flora McGee." Ned seemed impervious to the girl's toe-tapping irritation. "Quite the talented little lady, Flora. Makes the

best waffles in Dawson and sings like a nightingale, don't you, girlie?"

"The waffles are twenty-five cents each. You want one or not?" Flora brandished her spatula as though she was about to swat flies or any other pesky creatures that came near her.

She'd be pretty, Tim thought, admiring her shiny chestnut curls and pale triangular face, if she didn't have such a sour expression.

"Be seeing you around, young fella. Tell your mother, Flora, I'm ready to leave when she is." Ned Mumby raised one hand and wandered off.

Tim turned back to Flora. She was still scowling.

"*I'll* have a waffle," he said, remembering the coin Jake had dropped into his hand back at Lake Bennett.

"Money first." Flora's hand was out. Not until the quarter was safely in her apron pocket did she set the waffle pan on the stove. The sizzle and pop of batter on the hot griddle made Tim's mouth water again. By the time she'd flipped the waffle onto a plate and poured syrup over it, he had to stop himself from grabbing it out of her hand. How long was it since he'd eaten food he hadn't made himself?

The waffle tasted wonderful. Tim was licking syrup from his fingers when Flora's "What're you doing here, anyway?" broke his concentration. "Don't know when I last set eyes on somebody my age."

He put his hand down to let Pal lick the last crumbs. "Prospecting," he said casually, "with my brother."

"Huh! Another fool expecting to scoop nuggets out of the creek. Well, there's thousands ahead of you. And not a one of you knows what he's doing."

"And I suppose *you* do."

"I was born on one claim, brought up on another, we're stuck with

a third and there's no more left. They've all been taken." The last was said triumphantly, as though she'd staked the lot herself.

"Sure we hope to strike it rich," Tim said. Then, nettled by her scornful look, added, "But that's not the only reason *I'm* here. I keep notes about everything. When I get back with my first-person account of this gold rush, I'll be able to write for any newspaper I choose."

Flora's eyes widened and Tim felt a moment of satisfaction. "Have you —" she started, when they heard a shout from along the street. "Flora! Flora! Come and give me a hand."

"That's my mother." Flora darted around the end of the stall. Just then, a man sauntered up. "Let's have two of yer best waffles, girlie." As Flora hesitated, Tim said, "I'll go," and he ran toward a woman struggling with a large sack that kept sliding off one shoulder.

"I'm Tim," he said, reaching for the sack.

"Those stupid men I hired," she burst out, as though Tim were an old friend. "They've dumped everything in the mud back there and taken off. Not enough money in it, they said."

"I'll help." By the time they'd stacked a dozen sacks of flour and beans in the shed behind the stall, Tim had heard about the McGees' roadhouse up in the hills and the four years they'd earned their keep cooking while Flora's father mined one claim after another. Then, just two months ago, on the best claim they'd ever had, Flora's father had died in an accident.

Tim was trying to think how to say he was sorry when Mrs. McGee snapped the lock on the shed and said, "Well, you're a good worker, I'll give you that. How would you like a job for the rest of the day? Fifty cents and a stack of waffles for your supper."

"Done." Tim was elated. Who knew when Roy would be back.

Mrs. McGee kept him busy all afternoon carting sacks of flour, beans, tea and canned milk bought at bargain prices from stalls along the river.

It was six o'clock when Mrs. McGee said, "There's one last load and then we'll have supper." She pressed a hand into the small of her back, stretched and sat down abruptly.

"Mother, you're tired. I'll fetch it."

"No! I don't want you out in that town alone."

"Tim will be with me — and Pal."

"We'll look after her." Tim gathered up Pal's lead.

Mrs. McGee still looked dubious.

"I know right where to go," Flora jumped in. "You rest. Come on, Tim."

Tim found himself almost running to keep up. The minute they were out of her mother's sight, Flora darted around the corner of a stall, up a lane and they were on Front Street.

"Hey, this isn't the right way," Tim panted beside her. "We're supposed to be . . ."

She turned, her face urgent. "It's just a quick detour. It won't take a minute." And when he frowned, she hurried on. "I never get into the town on my own now that all these men are here. There's something important I have to do. And I've something to show you, too. Come on." As she spoke she was towing Tim along the boardwalk, darting between dawdling pedestrians.

"Here's the place *you* want." She was pointing at the newspaper office.

"The Klondike Nugget?" It took Tim a moment to realize she expected him to go in. He felt himself go hot.

"What do you have to lose? Everything in town's new. Everyone's looking for help. Might as well be you as the next one."

Tim glanced again at the sign. His heart was pounding. Sure, he'd dreamed about writing for a newspaper, but not yet. Not right this minute. The thought of showing anyone the disjointed jottings in his journal made him squirm.

Flora had run out of patience. "While you're making up your mind, I'm going over there."

She pointed at a building that rose a whole story above its squat neighbors. It was so new that its lapped boards weren't even painted, and the windows across its broad front were fitted with cheesecloth instead of glass. Bold letters stretching across the third floor announced "Fairview Hotel."

Tim was horrified. "You can't go there." In the few days he'd been in Dawson he'd heard the whole story of Belinda Mulrooney's magnificent hotel. Every steamer that docked brought more elegant goods to furnish it — chandeliers, silk drapes, silver cutlery and fine china. It was even going to have electricity. The likes of Tim Olsen and Flora McGee would certainly not be welcome there. But Flora was already picking her way across the muddy street, skirts held high. Reluctantly, Tim squelched after her.

Sounds of hammering and sawing grew louder as Flora pushed open the door. Carpenters were working flat out to have the hotel ready for its opening in two weeks' time. Flora stopped to scrub her muddy boot soles on the mat inside the door, and Tim sidled in after her, his hand clutching Pal's collar, keeping the dog close to his side.

He could see by the glossy bar along the length of one wall that they were in the saloon. A workman, his saw halfway through a plank, stared as Flora marched across the room to a woman standing, magnificent in burgundy silk, in front of a floor-length mirror. Before the woman could open her mouth, Flora was in full spate.

"Excuse me for interrupting, Miss Mulrooney, but I heard you were planning entertainment and I just wanted to let you know that I have an excellent singing voice. And I know a great many suitable songs. I see you have a piano. I could audition right now. Would you like to hear 'Home, Sweet Home' or 'I'm Only a Bird in a Gilded Cage'?" Finally she paused for breath. As Belinda Mulrooney appraised her through narrowed eyes, Flora pulled herself up tall. Tim was amazed to hear her add, "I'm fifteen and an experienced performer."

Miss Mulrooney tilted her head to one side, her lips pursed. Then a small smile broke the severity of her look. "Now I know who you are. Florence McGee's girl, right? And fifteen, you're not. I think you'd better skip along home — fast. You know as well as I do that Florence would have my head if I encouraged her daughter to go on the stage."

"But —"

"And don't you dare give your mother the idea that I invited you here."

"But this is a respectable hotel."

"Right. And I'm keeping it that way. Now, off you go, my girl. I want you out of here this instant."

From the set of Flora's shoulders, Tim expected her to flounce out, but she surprised him. "Yes, Miss Mulrooney," she said and walked quietly toward the door.

"Don't say one word," she said through clenched teeth once they were both outside. "Not one!" Ignoring the mud splattering her skirts, she stalked across the street and climbed onto the boardwalk.

They were nearly back at the laneway before Flora's purposeful march slowed down. "Well," she said finally, "it was worth a try."

"What *was* all that about being fifteen and an experienced entertainer?"

"Don't tell," she said. It didn't sound like a plea. More like an order.

"Of course not." He felt affronted and made no effort to keep the sharpness out of his voice.

Flora gave a big sigh and stopped walking. "It's the money," she said finally. "Money to get out of here. My aunt in Toronto is willing to have us live with her. But my mother won't hear of it. Not as poor relations, she says. If we can't pay our own way, we don't go."

"But you've got a claim. What about that?"

"If we don't work it, we lose it. Since my father died, it's just sitting there. Mother has plans to put a foreman in and hire men, but who knows if it'll be worth it." Flora had started walking again as she talked. Now they turned down the lane toward the river. "All we can count on is the roadhouse. Feeding miners earns us enough to live on but not enough to set up in Toronto. And if we don't go to Toronto, I'll never get to study music. It'll take gold from the claim to get us out of the North — unless I can use my voice. I know I could earn money that way, I just know it."

The fierceness in Flora's voice unsettled Tim. He had dreams, sure, but had he ever been so determined?

By the time Tim had had supper with the McGees and helped them bundle up all the provisions ready for tomorrow's trip to the roadhouse, he knew it must be nearly midnight. But the sky was still light when he and Pal finally set off for the scow, and small groups stood chatting at street corners. Would he ever get used to this eternal daylight? As he threaded his way among boats tied six deep along the shore, he spotted a form hunched on one end of their scow. Roy was back.

Tim's early-morning anger swirled up again. Roy must have heard him jumping from the deck of one boat to the deck of the next boat. He looked up with bloodshot eyes.

"Sorry, kid." His voice was croaky with tiredness. "It was all a swizzle. Didn't even get halfway there when I met guys coming back. Friends of the gold commissioner were up staking two days ago. Not a square foot left." The words came out in a fast monotone. "Be out of money soon." He cast a quick look at Tim, then turned away. "Looks like we're finished."

Tim stared at his brother. He could tell by the sagging shoulders that Roy's spunk was gone. He looked beat, just the way he had back in Seattle the day he'd had to tell Aunt Rachel he'd lost the store and his inheritance with it. What were they going to do now? Tim had a sudden vision of them ripping apart the scow to build their own stall on the beach, selling off the gear they'd lugged all those torturous miles, giving Mrs. McGee bargain prices on their flour and beans.

"We can't just give up."

But Roy wasn't listening. "Got to sleep." His mumbling grew less and less distinct as he dragged himself into the cabin of the scow and collapsed, still dressed, on his bedroll.

We can't just give up, Tim told himself. In the half-light that passed for night in the northern summer he hunched close to Pal for warmth. As the clatter of activity died around him and other inmates of scow city settled down to sleep, Tim thought and thought. Finally, having come to a decision, he dozed off himself.

When Tim woke, Roy was still sleeping, spread-eagled half out of his bedroll, snoring. Tim penciled directions to the McGees' waffle stand on a bag of flour near Roy's head, then he and Pal took off.

It was several hours before Roy showed up. Tim had had time to sound out Mrs. McGee on his plan and help load the mules she had hired for the trek back to the roadhouse. He and Flora were struggling to secure the last load with a diamond hitch knot, when Roy came shambling up. You might at least have shaved, was Tim's first thought. Not that Roy looked any scruffier than half the men in town.

Mrs. McGee put her hands on her hips and looked Roy up and down. "Your brother tells me you're a good worker," she said, not waiting for an introduction. Tim saw Roy's eyebrows snap up and decided not to meet his eyes.

"I've a business proposal for you," she continued crisply. "I've a claim needs working. I've hired a foreman who knows the work, but I need another strong back. If you're as good a worker as your brother is . . ." Roy shifted uncomfortably under Mrs. McGee's direct gaze. "Here are the terms. I'm not paying straight wages. Mining's a gamble. So we're sharing the risk. Right now our dump is paying eight cents a pan. Not much, but it'll carry us through the summer. My husband was convinced the drift was richer. It'll take a winter's work to find out. So the deal is Flora and I as owners get half, you and the foreman share the other half. Ask around if you want. It's as fair a deal as anyone will offer you."

Roy shuffled his feet again. "I suppose Tim's told you I had no luck out at Dominion Creek?"

Mrs. McGee paused for a moment. When she spoke again, her voice was softer. "This is a hard country. And right now it's overrun with fools and scoundrels. Good men can get trampled in the rush."

Roy nodded. "Your offer sounds fair." Then, after a long pause, "As you say, we're all gamblers here. Thank you for the chance."

Tim looked at Flora. Was he imagining it or was she glad that he and Roy would be going with them?

Maybe they wouldn't be picking nuggets out of the creek, but they'd be on a claim, a working claim. Maybe they'd find gold. And for sure, he'd be filling his journal. And maybe, once he had some experience on a claim, maybe he'd write something up for the *Klondike Nugget*. Maybe he just would.

DAWSON

July 8, 1898

Mud everywhere! I've changed my trail boots for rubber boots like everyone else in town. The minute I step off the boardwalk — and it's pretty narrow — I'm in muck halfway to my knees. Even so, there are people everywhere, just milling about, their boots and pants almost white with dried mud after a walk down Front Street.

In July 1898, when Tim and Roy arrived, Dawson was a town rapidly growing into a city. Front Street, the main business street, was a jumble of small log buildings and larger clapboard ones, some with tall false fronts to make them look more impressive. Day after day, work gangs hammered and sawed, throwing up buildings as quickly as the still-green lumber arrived from the sawmills. Many were saloons and dance halls for the entertainment of miners who came in from their claims with a full poke (leather pouch) of gold. But Dawson had the services a city needs as well — a hospital, five churches, two banks and two newspapers. No matter what the sign outside promised, inside, most buildings were little more than small, dark, often dirty shacks.

When the main flood of stampeders came floating down the Yukon, they rushed into town looking for places to stay. Streets became lined with crude cabins, tents — any structure that would shelter the newcomers. These "homes" spread over the flats and flowed up the side of the Midnight Dome, the hill that loomed over the town.

By the time Tim and Roy arrived, there was no room left. So, like hundreds of others, they lived on their scow. Boats were tied six deep for 3 km (2 mi.) along the river. The only way to get to shore was by jumping from deck to deck.

Dawson's growth had happened quickly. Just two years before, the area had been swampy land used by the Han people as a fishing camp. But when gold was discovered on the Klondike, a trader named Joe Ladue realized that miners would soon be flooding into the area. Anyone providing them with goods could make a fortune, and Ladue intended to be that person.

Where the Klondike River empties into the Yukon River, Ladue staked out a townsite he called Dawson, after George M. Dawson, director of the Geological Survey of Canada, who visited the Yukon in the 1880s. Then he set up a sawmill. Before long he was selling town lots and lumber to the miners who were striking it rich in the hills above the town.

Dawson grew slowly in 1897. But soon it exploded into a city of more than 30 000. In its heyday Dawson was as big as Winnipeg was at the time and only slightly smaller than Seattle.

E.A Hegg's photograph shows the restless crowds roaming the muddy streets of Dawson.

NATIVE PEOPLE

The swampy plain that became the city of Dawson was not an empty piece of wilderness when Joe Ladue decided to build there. For thousands of years the Athapaskan Han people had fished and hunted along the shores of the Klondike and Yukon Rivers. Their largest fishing camp was at the mouth of the river they called Thron-diuck.

This place was important to the Han. Each fall herds of migrating caribou forded the river nearby. And each fall, for as long as the elders of the community could remember, hunters had culled the herds to supply their families with winter meat and skins to make clothes.

By the 1870s and 1880s the Han were meeting a few prospectors in the hills above their Thron-diuck River. After 1896 that trickle of prospectors became a flood and the Native people found themselves pushed out of their fishing camp. They retreated 5 km (3 mi.) downstream to the mouth of Moosehide Creek, but flight didn't help. As the prospectors spread along the rivers and up the valleys searching for gold, they stripped the hillsides of trees. Wildlife moved away in search of new sources of food and shelter. Without wood for fires and caribou for meat, the Han were soon weakened by starvation and disease. In less than seven years their entire way of life had been radically changed.

BUYING AND SELLING

July 9, 1898

Saw a real sourdough today — that's what the locals call someone who's spent a winter here. I thought he was a hobo at first — he was dressed all in tatters. But I knew he was a prospector as soon as he pulled his poke out of his pocket.

Prospectors and miners in Dawson paid for things with gold dust. Every store had a small gold scale on the counter. To buy something, a customer produced his poke full of gold dust and a small tin scoop called a blower. He shoveled a little dust onto one pan of the scale and the storekeeper piled weights on the other until the scale balanced at the agreed-upon price. In 1898, 28 g (1 oz.) of gold dust (about the size of a sugar cube) was worth $16 in Dawson.

Some freewheeling types just threw their pokes on the counter and said, "Help yourself." And some less-than-honest storekeepers did just that. They grew their fingernails long or wet their fingertips just before they took a pinch of gold dust (the usual price for a drink in a saloon) so that they could scoop more than the proper amount.

Gold dust scattered easily, so every storekeeper set his scales on a velvet cloth. After closing time he shook out the cloth just to make sure he got every grain of gold. He even "panned" the sawdust on the floor. It could yield as much as $20 a night if customers had been careless.

WOMEN IN THE KLONDIKE

Florence McGee knew what many women coming to the Klondike learned — money could be made by selling the miners what they couldn't make for themselves. Many women went into business once they discovered how much time and hard work it would take before a claim would pay out. Some set up laundries or bakeries. Several who'd had the foresight to bring sewing machines made tidy livings as seamstresses. But the women who struck it rich had bigger ideas than providing domestic services.

BELINDA MULROONEY, ENTREPRENEUR

In July 1898, Belinda Mulrooney opened the biggest hotel in Dawson. To a city of log cabins and mud she brought linen tablecloths, cut-glass chandeliers, fancy furniture and a French chef. The miners who had struck it rich, the Kings of the Klondike as they were called, were happy to spend their gold dust in Belinda's Fairview Hotel.

Belinda started out small. She was a coal-miner's daughter from Pennsylvania with an eye for a good business deal. In 1890, at age 18, she left home and three years later opened a restaurant at the Chicago World's Fair. By 1896 she had sensed the promise of the North and was managing a ladies clothing store in Juneau, Alaska. When gold was discovered in the neighboring Klondike, Belinda invested in hot-water bottles and silk goods, then headed for Dawson. Within days she had sold them for a huge profit.

Belinda's motto was simple: Find out what people want and give it to them. Miners who had slogged all winter out on the claims wanted a warm meal and a clean bed. Belinda gave them both. In 1897, she built a hotel in the heart of the richest gold country, right where Eldorado Creek met Bonanza Creek. The miners loved it and as they stood around the bar gossiping, Belinda picked up useful information about valuable claims. Soon she was investing her profits in gold mines.

As thousands of stampeders flooded into Dawson, she decided *that* was the place to be. In July 1898, at the height of the stampede, she not only opened her elegant Fairview Hotel, she also invested in a telephone company and the Hygiea Water Company to supply the town with safe water.

Belinda had many adventures in her long, long life but it was the Klondike that made her rich and famous. She was one of its most successful businesspeople.

DANCE-HALL GIRLS

Men who'd spent months working long, hard hours on their claims certainly wanted warm food and clean beds, but they also wanted entertainment. This the women of the dance halls provided. Many girls and young women made the arduous journey to Dawson in the hopes of making their fortune on the stage. And men starved for a little fun were willing to reward even moderately talented singers and dancers who brightened their lives, if only for an evening.

Sisters Polly and Lottie Oatley opened their own concert hall, where they sang sentimental songs to homesick miners. After each set of songs, the audience threw nuggets of gold onto the stage to show their appreciation. Between performances, the sisters came down off the stage and danced with miners for a dollar a dance.

The Oatleys were successful but they never became as popular as Cad Wilson. She wasn't pretty but she had a way with a song. Her audiences were so enthusiastic that after each performance, she swept a fortune in gold dust off the stage. Then, when she decided to return home, the miners presented her with a belt made of nuggets. The buckle was cast in the shape of a gold pan and in it were a gold pick, shovel and bucket.

An even bigger hit was nine-year-old Margie Newman. Miners lonely for their families broke down and cried when she sang about home in a high, sweet voice or, dressed in tartan, danced the Highland fling. By the end of her act the stage was covered in gold dust and nuggets.

Successful entertainers left Dawson rich. However, many of the young women hoping to sing and dance their way to fame and fortune became dance-hall girls. From 6:00 p.m. to 6:00 a.m. every night except Sunday, they worked for a dollar a dance. Although they brought a little glamour and companionship into the lives of lonely miners, their own lives were often filled with despair. Worn out by poor food and long hours, many died of tuberculosis. Others returned south, no richer than when they arrived.

GAMBLING

July 9, 1898

Saw Jake this evening. I yelled for him to wait up but he disappeared into a hotel. I followed him into a dark, smoky room. Must have been part of a dance hall — someone was playing the piano. The man behind the bar yelled at me, "Hey, you! Get out of here. No kids allowed." I wonder what Jake was up to?

Chances are Jake was headed for the room behind the dance hall, the room where gambling took place. Gambling was a big part of life in Dawson. Miners who had worked long, lonely months on the claim came into town looking for companionship and thrills. These they found with the dollar-a-dance girls and in the crowded gaming saloons.

The two most popular games, roulette and faro, took no skill. Winning was strictly a matter of chance. At the faro table, the dealer laid out cards and the players bet on which face card would appear first. In roulette, miners traded their gold for yellow discs called chips. "Place your bets," shouted the dealer, and the players put a stack of chips on either a red or black segment of the wheel. Then the dealer spun the wheel, and the players waited for it to stop. If it stopped on a player's color, he won. If not, he lost.

In many mining towns the wheels were crooked, rigged so that the players seldom won. In Dawson, the Mounties kept the wheel honest. But even so, gambling could lead to disaster. Many men couldn't stop once they began losing. The next spin of the wheel, they felt, would be their lucky one. So they kept putting down chips until they'd gambled away all the proceeds of a season's hard work.

Gambling provided excitement for more than just the players. When someone was on a winning streak or had bet his claim against the throw of the dice, crowds gathered to watch. They could hardly believe their eyes the night Ed Mahon, owner of the Monte Carlo Hotel, bet everything he owned on one turn of the cards — and lost. Another night a gambler named One-Eyed Riley had a winning streak that brought him $28 000. Determined to leave the Klondike with a fortune, he headed for Skagway, Alaska, and the next boat out. But he made the mistake of stepping into a gambling hall while he waited. In less than an hour, he lost every cent on three tosses of the dice. For men like Riley, gambling was as exciting as the search for gold. Fortunes changed hands regularly in the smoky, dimly lit rooms behind the dance halls.

Diamond Hitch Knot

Tim was helping Flora with a diamond hitch knot. He had learned it from one of the stampeders who told him it was the best way to fasten an awkward load to the back of a mule. Here's how to tie a diamond hitch.

You'll need:
plywood or particle board approximately
  20 cm x 25 cm (8 in. x 10 in.)
6 cup hooks
2 books
3 m (10 ft.) of heavy string, twine or cord

1. Screw a cup hook into each corner of the board and also into the center point of the 20 cm (8 in.) sides. Place the 2 books in the middle of the board. This will be your "load."

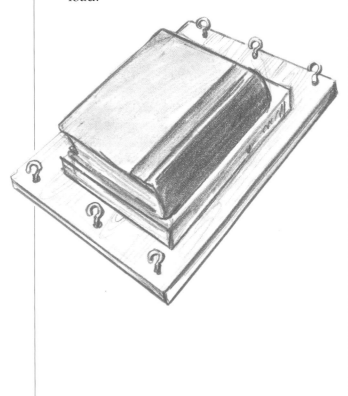

2. Tie one end of the cord to hook # 1. Pull the cord around hook # 2. Return it to the first hook and loop it around once to secure it.

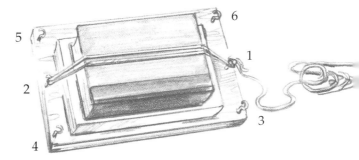

3. Take one line in each hand. Twist one line over the other at least ten times.

4. Pull the two lines apart into a diamond shape.

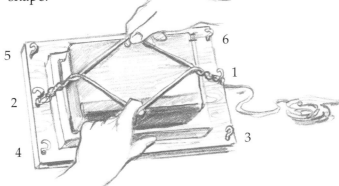

5. Hook the free end of the cord around hook # 3, then loop it through the diamond and down around hook #4.

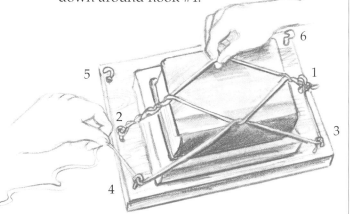

6. Bring the end back up through the diamond again, then hook the cord around hook #5.

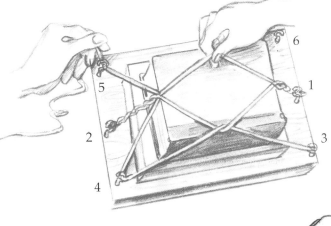

7. Bring the end back up through the diamond again and hook it around hook #6.

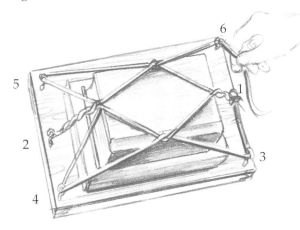

8. Pull it tight, then tie the cord to hook #1.

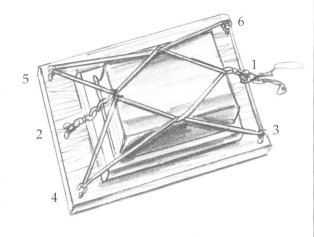

SUMMER ON
THE DIGGINGS

July 10, 1898

Here's real news! The foreman Mrs. McGee hired is Ned Mumby, who helped me get Pal up the Golden Stairs. He grew up on mining claims during the Cariboo Gold Rush and fancied trying his hand again.

We stopped at the McGees' roadhouse to help unload the mules. It's not what I expected — just a log cabin with a low, sloping roof. It's covered in sod and they grow lettuce and cabbages on it! Miners come in for homecooked meals or to sit around and chat. Some get a 5-pound pail filled with baked beans to take back to their camp. Lots of miners can't be bothered cooking for themselves, Flora says.

July 11, 1898

On the claim, at last! I thought we'd be alone out here in the bush, but there're cabins and mining operations as far as I can see all up and down the creek. Not much activity, though. Ned says wait until spring when everyone's washing gravel like mad. Only our claim still has a dump. That's gravel from the winter digging.

Our cabin is tiny. Three of us and only two narrow bunks, so my first job is cutting some saplings to make a frame for my bed. It'll be quite a squeeze, but four miners are crammed into the cabin next over, so I guess we can't complain.

July 20, 1898

According to Ned, we've got to wash a lot of gravel if we want to take more than a laborer's wage out of here. We're using a gadget called a rocker. It's just a wooden box set on crosswise rockers. One of us shovels gravel into the box and then ladles water over it. A sieve in the box catches all the large pieces of gravel. The sand and gold wash down onto a mat. It works but it's slow. Ned says once we get the sluice boxes up and running it'll be lots faster.

August 5, 1898

Flora and Mrs. McGee were here today. They come once a week to check on the gold. Roy was annoyed the first time, but Ned said Mrs. McGee's got no reason to trust us — we're little better than strangers to her. Anyway, she knows her way around mining in this country, which is more than we do. I've decided that Ned is a peaceable man. I like that word. Peaceable. I like the feeling, too.

Back and forth. Push and pull. Hour after hour. Tim gave one final shove on the rocker's upright handle. The second he stopped moving, a whining swarm of mosquitoes descended. He spat out a mouthful. I'll never get used to this. On the river drifting down to Dawson, they were bad enough, but here! And as for gold, how could I have been stupid enough to think it was just lying around on the ground? Well I sure know better now.

He'd been working all morning, shoveling gravel into the wooden box, ladling in water from a pail, then rocking the box back and forth to shake the gold to the bottom. Between working the rocker and lugging the pails of water, he ached all over, and every inch of him itched from the angry bites.

Tim waved one hand in front of his face to swat away the swarm and glanced up the hill to where Ned and Roy were working. He could see the steady rise and fall of their pickaxes as they dug a ditch to run water from a spring Ned had dammed farther up the rise.

Better get on with it. Don't want Roy to think I can't do my share. He'd sieved another four shovelfuls through when Pal's head shot up. With a "woof," the dog was on his feet, bounding down the narrow trail that bordered the creek. Tim squinted after him and caught the flutter of a blue skirt. Flora, weighed down by two heavy pails, was trudging uphill toward him. Beans, I'll bet. Part of Mrs. McGee's roadhouse business was cooking for miners. They supplied the dried beans and she baked up large batches and packed them into empty butter pails. But where on earth was Flora headed?

Tim ran down the trail and grabbed a pail from her.

"Thanks," she panted. "Hot today."

"How come you're lugging these up here? I thought the miners came down for them?"

"Not old man Brennan." Flora dipped her handkerchief into the bucket of water and mopped her face right through the mosquito netting draped over her hat and tied under her chin. "Pays extra to have his delivered. Afraid someone'll rob him if he leaves his claim. As if he had anything worth stealing."

Except his gold, Tim thought. He was amazed at how miners left jars full of gold dust sitting around. He'd expected Ned to hide theirs even though they had only half a tobacco tin of coarse granules. After all, getting even that much had taken hours and hours of hard work. But Ned just put it up on a shelf in plain sight.

Tim set down Flora's pail of beans just as Roy came sliding down the slope. All he said was "Too much for you, is it?" and nodded at the abandoned rocker. Tim flushed when he saw Flora's eyes widen.

Ned made matters worse. Clumping down the hill, he spotted Flora's heavy pails. "Hot day to be delivering beans," he said. "Maybe Tim here could help you out."

Roy was bent over the rocker inspecting the sludge. "Yeah. Might as well." He sounded disgusted. "You're sure not doing much here."

I'm doing my best, Tim wanted to shout. Instead, he grabbed a pail and took off up the trail without a word to anyone.

"Everything I do is wrong!" he burst out to Flora when she caught up with him. "What's the matter with him, anyway?"

"Maybe he's worried." Flora stopped to catch her breath, and Tim realized he'd been almost running up the slope.

"Worried? Sure, there's lots to worry about, but does he have to take it out on me?"

Flora interrupted his thoughts. "How much gold are you getting out of the dump?" She picked up her pail and started walking, more slowly this time.

"Not much more than when you were here last. About half a tobacco tin so far."

"My father was so sure he'd found a good paystreak."

Tim gave her a quick sideways glance. It was the first time she'd mentioned her father. "Ned says once we have the sluice set up it'll go faster."

"Father was building it this spring." Flora paused. Her voice went quiet, so quiet Tim had to strain to hear. "It was just then that he . . ." She turned her face away. "It was all my fault."

"*Your* fault?"

"He worked the claim alone. Every couple of days one of us would bring him fresh bread and beans. It was my turn, that day. I called for him but no one answered." She swallowed, then continued. "I wasn't worried — I thought he'd gone off to help someone. And . . . and it was cold. I wanted to get home."

She stopped walking and looked off into the distance. Her voice was flat when she continued. "Next day, Mother came up with me. She . . . she found him at the bottom of the shaft. He'd knocked himself out. That's why he couldn't call for help." Flora took off her hat and rubbed her sleeve across her eyes. "Maybe he was still alive when I was there. He died of exposure, they said."

Tim shuddered. Frozen to death.

"I hate this place," Flora broke out. "We have to get out of here. We just have to."

Tim didn't know what to say. He offered the first thought that came to him. "I'm sure there's lots of gold. Look what we managed with just the rocker. And Ned says we'll really see those jars filling once we've got the sluice working."

Flora just shrugged.

They walked on in silence, then he tried again. "This is a heck of a climb. How often do you deliver to old man Brennan, anyway?"

"Every two or three weeks." She seemed relieved by the change of topic. "He doesn't let me set foot on the claim, y'know. Even threatened me with his shotgun the first time. That got Mother good and riled. Told him if either of us ever saw that gun again, it was the end of the baked beans."

They'd left most of the diggings far behind by the time they reached the line Mr. Brennan had blazed to mark his claim.

No chunk-chunk of a shovel at work, Tim noted. He peered about warily. "Seems awfully quiet." He wouldn't put it past the old man to jump out from behind his cabin waving a shotgun, no matter what Mrs. McGee had said to him.

"Must be nearly noon. Maybe he's eating. Mr. Brennan?" Flora called. "We've brought your beans." They listened for a reply, Tim with a hand on Pal's collar just in case old man Brennan didn't like dogs, either.

"Sluice is dry." Tim craned his neck to look, keeping his toes firmly behind the boundary line. "Can't have done any work this morning."

"Gone to town, maybe." Although that didn't seem likely.

Tim hunkered down beside Pal, searching for clues among the usual untidy clutter of a digging. Up the slope stood a tiny cabin, shovel and pickax leaning to one side of its open door. Couldn't have gone far, Tim decided. Piles of gravel covered the rest of the site. Sticking out of the largest pile was cribbing that boxed the mouth of a shaft. That was where he should be working.

Pal tugged free and loped off to nose around the smaller gravel piles that marked abandoned shafts. Tim caught a sharp whiff of whiskey just as Flora pointed to a smashed jug. Then Pal gave several short barks. He was standing by an abandoned shaft.

Tim ran. At the bottom of the hole he could dimly see what looked like a pile of crumpled clothes. "Mr. Brennan? Are you hurt?"

No sound. Was he breathing? Hard to tell from this height. "Flora, we'll have to . . ." Tim turned. Flora was still standing at the edge of the claim, rigid, her face white.

Tim ran back to her. "Flora?"

"He's dead, isn't he?"

"I can't tell. We'll have to . . ."

"I . . . I have to get out of here."

"Flora! We can't just leave him."

"I c-can't." Her voice rose thin and panicky. With one more wild-eyed glance in the direction of the shaft, she turned and ran.

Tim watched her stumble and trip down the trail. What can I do on my own? He looked back at the shaft, then reluctantly returned and peered down again.

"Mr. Brennan?" Tim lay flat out on the ground and reached over the edge. No good. Too far down. A ladder. I need a ladder. He was scrambling up to look for one when he heard a faint groan. The bundle stirred and half turned over. Eyes stared up from the gloom.

For a second Tim was too startled to say anything. Then he shouted, "Are you hurt?!"

The old man took a long, rattling breath. "I'm alive," he croaked. "And I sure ain't deaf."

"I'll get you some water."

"No! Me jug." The bundle stirred again, tried to push up on one arm, then collapsed with a groan.

"Don't worry, Mr. Brennan. I'll get help."

"Not them Haggartys!" the old man screeched. "No way them thievin' Haggartys're settin' foot on my claim." He struggled into a sitting position and growled, "Ah, me ankle. It's painin' me somethin' fierce."

His loud wheezing alarmed Tim. "Stay calm, Mr. Brennan. We'll have you out in no time."

Tim quickly rounded up a ladder, a coil of rope and a tin mug full of water. Back at the hole, he looped one end of the rope into a harness and knotted it around Pal's chest. "I'm going to need your help, Pal," he said, slinging the rest of the coil over his shoulder. He wrestled the ladder into the shaft. It bounced and swayed as he descended.

Down in the shaft, the air had a stale chilliness. A stench riper than spilled whiskey rose to meet him, and his stomach lurched. Mr. Brennan was curled on his side. Had he passed out again? Well, maybe that would make it easier to get the rope around him.

The fetid smell was making Tim gag. He averted his face, hoping for fresher air as he worked at knotting the rope. By the time he had it securely cinched, the old man was stirring again. Tim slid the mug of water out of reach of the thrashing arms.

"What d'ye think yer doin'? Leave off this clobber, will 'ee?" The old miner was pushing himself into a sitting position and grabbing at the rope all at the same time.

"Have some water, Mr. Brennan, then we'll try the ladder." The old man snatched the mug and drank noisily. "Ladder. That'll do 'er," was all he said.

The water seemed to have perked him up. Without any prompting from Tim, he grasped a rung of the ladder and pulled himself slowly onto his one good foot. By the lantern light, Tim noticed that Mr. Brennan's hands were torn and bleeding. He must have tried to claw his way up the frozen muck of the walls.

"Tim?" At the sound of the voice from above, Tim's head jerked up.

"Flora! Help Pal keep that rope taut, will you?"

As the rope tightened, Tim shouted, "We're coming up!" At least, here's hoping. But now that Mr. Brennan was on his feet, he seemed to catch on. With Tim boosting and Flora and Pal tugging, the old man pulled himself up the ladder, hopping from rung to rung on his good foot. Then, with a final heave from Tim, he pulled himself over the edge and collapsed, panting on the muddy ground. "Thirty years a miner," he groaned, "and I fall down me own abandoned shaft."

But the job wasn't done yet. It took both Tim and Flora to get Mr. Brennan, half hobbling, half hopping, to the stool beside the cabin door. He looked so white by the time he flopped down that Tim blurted out, "I . . . I'd better stay a day or two. 'Til you're on your feet again." He caught Flora's incredulous look. I know, he wanted to shout, but how else will he manage?

Mr. Brennan had been poking gingerly at his ankle. "No need. No need. Just a sprain. Cut me a forked stick for a crutch, will 'ee? That and those beans'll do me fine."

Tim hoped the relief didn't show on his face. "I'll call back tomorrow and see how you're doing."

"Suit yourself." The old man was bent over, rubbing his ankle. Even when they propped the crutch beside him and left, he didn't seem to notice.

As they started down the trail, Flora said, "I'm sorry. I just couldn't face —"

"Never mind. You came back. I couldn't have got him out without you."

"You seemed to be doing just fine. As though you'd dealt with mine accidents all your life."

Tim shrugged off the praise, but he felt a warm glow nonetheless. To have someone as capable as Flora say he'd done a good job . . . That was worth something.

The next day, when Tim and Pal climbed the valley to check on Mr. Brennan, Tim was surprised to find the old prospector sitting outside panning in a large tub of water.

"It's you then, is it?" Without looking up, the old man kept dipping, then swirling the pan. "Smart thinkin' yesterday. Seem to have a good head on your shoulders — fer a young feller. Shame to waste it." He peered into the pan, stirring the gravel with one finger. "You can get trapped in this country, y'know. Always moving on to the next valley. Always hoping for the next big strike."

He gave the pan a swirl that washed the last of the gravel into the tub. "Hah! Look at this." He beckoned impatiently.

Tim glanced into the pan. Black sand. Nothing unusual about that. Then he saw something glitter. Mr. Brennan was picking out lumps of gold. He grabbed Tim's hand. "There's one for you, one for the girl — much help she was, but never mind." He was counting nuggets the size of grapes into Tim's palm. "And one for the dog."

Tim closed his hand around the three nuggets and stared in astonishment at the old miner, who was already scooping out another panful of sludge to wash.

"That's us quits then," growled the old man. "But you keep bringin' me m'beans, y'hear? And don't forget what else I said." He cocked one beady eye at Tim. "Mind the country don't trap 'ee — like it's done others not a long spit from here."

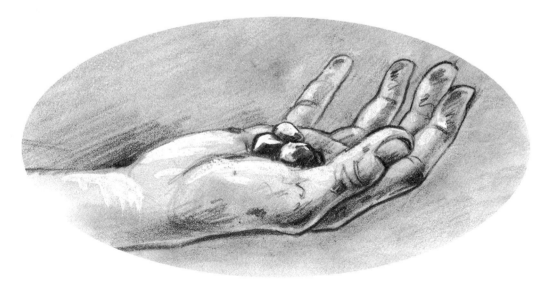

FINDING GOLD

Gold is a mineral that forms veins in rock such as granite or quartz. A vein that is wide and runs for a good distance is called a lode. To get at the lode, miners must dig shafts and tunnels into the rock, grind up the gold-bearing rock and then melt it in a furnace to retrieve the gold. This takes many men using expensive equipment.

But in some parts of North America, especially in streambeds along the Pacific coast, natural forces such as earthquakes, glaciers and floods grind up the rock and wash the gold into streams. On its journey downstream, the gold tumbles with the waterborne gravel. Sometimes it is rounded into nuggets. The nugget that started off the gold rush was as big around as a man's thumb. More often the gold is pulverized into flakes or fine dust called flour gold. The heavy gold sinks to the bed of the river.

Gold released by natural forces is called placer gold. Experienced miners knew that placer gold in a stream or riverbed could mean more gold nearby. This is because, over thousands of years, rivers and streams change course, leaving their gold-rich gravel beds hidden under many meters or feet of earth and gravel. So miners looked for signs of placer gold as they panned the streams and rivers, then started digging nearby to find more.

shaft

earth and gravel

old river bed

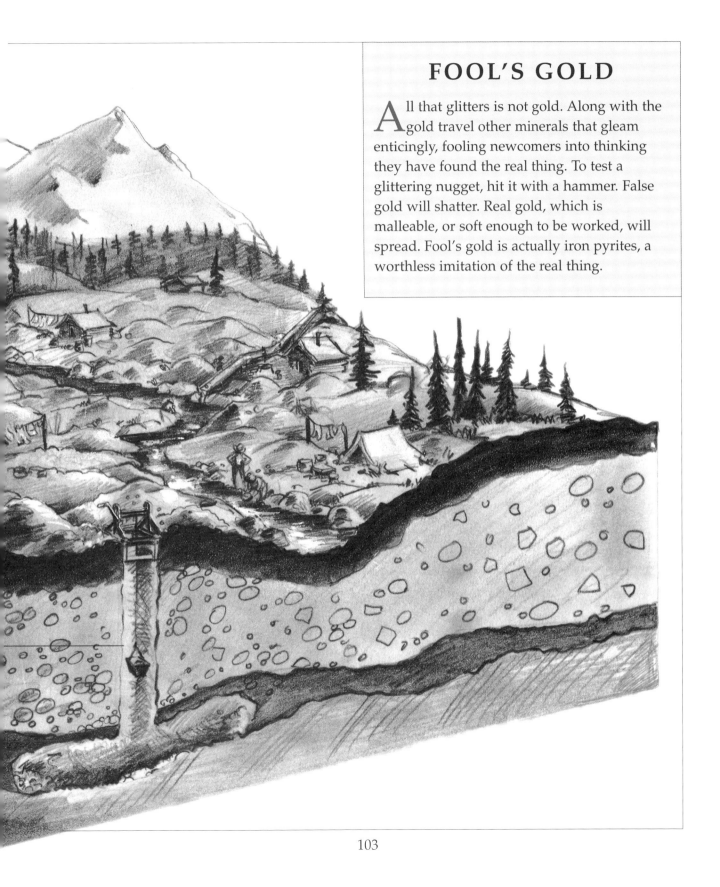

FOOL'S GOLD

All that glitters is not gold. Along with the gold travel other minerals that gleam enticingly, fooling newcomers into thinking they have found the real thing. To test a glittering nugget, hit it with a hammer. False gold will shatter. Real gold, which is malleable, or soft enough to be worked, will spread. Fool's gold is actually iron pyrites, a worthless imitation of the real thing.

PANNING FOR GOLD

July 12, 1898

Panning isn't as easy as it looks. My feet are ready to drop off from standing in freezing cold water and my back aches from hunching over. But I did get a few grains of gold — about 2¢ worth, Ned reckons. He says this is called poor man's gold. No fancy equipment is needed — even an old frying pan would do.

Tim was learning how to pan creek or river gravel to test for gold. Most miners used a pan with a wide, flat bottom and sloping sides. Into this they scooped the gravel and sand from the stream or riverbed, added a little water and began to swirl it. As the light sand and gravel washed out, the remaining solids would sort themselves from lightest to heaviest. Since gold is 19.3 times heavier than water, it sinks to the bottom.

After picking out the larger pieces of gravel, a miner examined what was left. At the bottom of the pan would probably be a few spoonfuls of black sand in which any gold would be hidden. Adding more water, a miner swirled ever more carefully. As the sand fanned out into a crescent, there at the tail end would be the "color" — a tiny trace of fine gold.

STAKING A CLAIM

Prospectors lucky enough to find a site with gold-bearing gravel had to make a legal claim before they could work it. The rules set out by the Government of Canada were strict. In 1896, a prospector was allowed to stake an area 150 m (500 ft.) wide, running 300 m (1000 ft.) back from the creek or river. By 1898, with thousands of gold seekers flooding into the Yukon, claims were reduced to 75 m (250 ft.) wide.

To stake a claim, the prospector marked it with four small posts with squared-off tops. On each of these posts, the prospector wrote "I claim 500 feet up [or down] the creek for mining purposes" and signed his name.

The mining registrar would give the claim a number. The first claim on any creek was called Discovery Claim and numbered 0. From then on, a claim was numbered by its location above or below Discovery.

Once a claim was staked, the prospector had only three days to register the claim at the office of the gold commissioner. A claim allowed the miner to cut timber and mine gold for one year. It didn't give him ownership of the site, but it *did* protect his right to mine that spot. Each year, to renew his license, he had to prove he was working the claim.

Old-time miners believed in sharing good news about a find, but they risked having their claim "jumped." An unscrupulous miner might replace another's stakes with his own, then race to the commissioner's office to register it first. The presence of the North-West Mounted Police kept claim jumping to a minimum.

GETTING THE GOLD

Panning a stream was a way to test a location for gold. If a place looked promising, the hard work began. In winter, when the ground was frozen, shafts were dug down and the gravel and dirt removed. In spring the gravel and dirt was "washed" to extract the gold it held. Washing was mostly done with a rocker or a sluice box.

THE ROCKER

A rocker (sometimes called a cradle) was a wooden box, about 1 m (3 ft.) long by 30 cm (1 ft.) wide, set on rockers. At the top was a removable tray with holes in the bottom, which acted as a sieve. The miner shoveled sand and gravel into this sieve, poured water over it and grabbed the handle to rock the box back and forth. The shaking forced the sand and gold through the sieve, leaving the larger gravel behind. Under the sieve, a canvas apron caught anything that dropped through. More rocking moved this material onto a slanted board with crosspieces called riffles. As water washed out the sand, the heavy gold was trapped by the riffles.

a tray with holes stopped the larger pieces of gravel from falling through

a canvas apron caught nuggets

wooden riffles trapped the fine gold

rockers

THE SLUICE BOX

A faster way to wash gravel was to set up a series of wooden troughs, each about 2 m (6 ft.) long, that fitted together to form a long, sloping sluice. The bottom was lined with matting, held down by wooden riffles. A miner shoveled sand and gravel into the upper end of the sluice. Water carried the material down the trough, washing the lighter debris out the lower end while the heavier gold was trapped by the riffles. At least once a day, the water was turned off and the riffles removed. The matting was lifted out and washed to retrieve the gold.

Operating a sluice box required a great deal of water. Because the Yukon receives very little rain, miners used two other sources: spring runoff from melting snow or water from creeks. They dug ditches to channel spring runoff and built dams to trap water in ponds for use later in the season. Some built flumes, wooden pipes that extended more than 1.6 km (1 mi.) up a valley to a source of water, such as a spring.

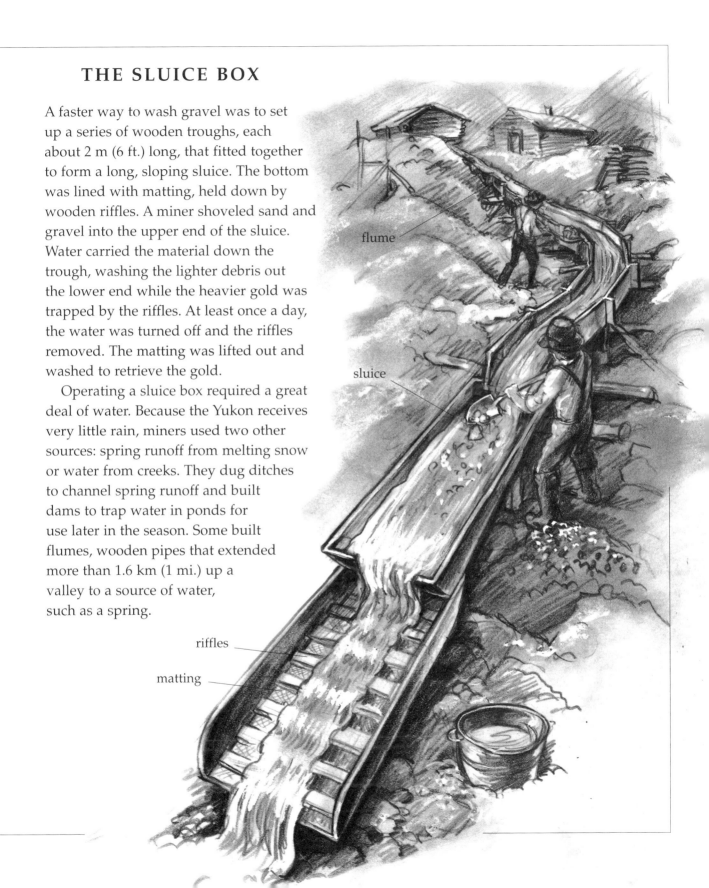

flume

sluice

riffles

matting

BONANZA!

The biggest gold rush in history started with a chance find. Late in the summer of 1896, George Carmack was roaming the Klondike wilderness with his wife, Kate, a woman of the Tagish nation, and her brothers, Skookum Jim Keish and Tagish Charley. In one of the creek valleys they ran into a prospector named Robert Henderson. As prospectors did, Henderson shared the news that there'd been a find on Gold Bottom Creek, a small river that emptied into the Klondike. But Carmack and the others were in need of ready money, so they ignored the tip and set off for Rabbit Creek, another tributary of the Klondike. There they planned to cut logs to sell to the sawmill downriver.

As they traveled up the creek, out of long habit they stopped every so often to pan for gold. The traces of color at the bottom of each pan were disappointing. Logging was obviously a surer way to make money. That evening, while cleaning their dishes in the stream, Jim Keish reached down and picked a large nugget from the bottom of the stream. In the crumbling rock of the stream bank more gold was visible.

Within minutes the men had panned 7 g (1/4 oz.) of gold, worth about $4. For prospectors happy to find 10¢ of gold at the bottom of a pan, this was an incredible amount. Flinging down their pans, they began shouting and dancing. They knew they had struck it rich.

Once the excitement wore off, Carmack and his partners panned enough coarse gold to fill an empty shotgun shell, as proof of their find. Then George Carmack convinced the others to let him stake the important "discovery" claim, which, he argued, no native person would be allowed to stake. The others finally agreed.

On the way to Forty Mile Creek to register the claims, they told everyone they met about their bonanza. People dropped what they were doing and rushed to the new strike. In Forty

Mile Creek, Carmack stopped first at the saloon. As men crowded around, he poured his shotgun shell full of gold on the scales and told his story. Within minutes the saloon had emptied.

The story spread like a bushfire. Men abandoned claims they'd been working all season and headed for Rabbit Creek. In no time at all, prospectors had staked every inch of the creek. And once they realized how rich it was, they gave it a new name — Bonanza! Bonanza Creek and its tributary, Eldorado, produced the richest claims in the Klondike — nearly $7 million worth of gold.

That summer of 1896 George Carmack, Jim Keish and Charley were too poor to work the claims. First they had to cut logs to earn enough money to buy the equipment needed to wash large amounts of gravel. But once they started, they cleaned up $1400 in less than a month. In all, they took hundreds of thousands of dollars from the claim.

After mining for two seasons, in the fall of 1898 Carmack took Jim and Charley, as well as Kate and his daughter Gracie "Outside" to visit his family. In Seattle he drove around in a carriage emblazoned with "George Carmack, Discoverer of the Gold in the Yukon." But the trip south was not a success. Kate felt bewildered by the city bustle, sneered at by her husband's relations and humiliated by the press, who loved to make fun of her "wilderness ways."

By 1900 Carmack had abandoned Kate and married again. Despite owning an estate worth $1.5 million, he refused to settle a penny on Kate. She lived out the rest of her life in the North, dependent on a government pension. Carmack invested his money and lived comfortably until his death in 1922. Jim Keish, the real discoverer of gold in the Yukon, could also have lived comfortably on the proceeds from his claim. But he preferred to live the hard life of a prospector. He died in 1916.

WINTER ON THE DIGGINGS

November 15, 1898

No time to write the past few months. Too busy. We've been working like mad digging the shaft. My job is carrying firewood. Every night we set a fire to thaw the frozen muck. The next day Ned and Roy dig it out. About 6 inches a day we're managing. They're down pretty far now, so they shovel the muck into a bucket and I winch it up and dump it.

December 10, 1898

Just learned a great new word — mushing. Mr. Brennan says that's what they call traveling over snow. It's mostly used by dogsledders. So now I shout "Mush!" to Pal when we go out. Ned says one day soon we'll mush in to Dawson for a change.

December 15, 1898

Mr. Brennan just left. We've sure seen a lot of him since his ankle healed. He and Roy get on like strange cat and dog. His usual greeting is "Himself's not here? Good." Then he peels off his outer layers and settles down for a pipe with Ned. Sometimes he plays cards with me, but if Roy's about, he's off again in no time. He says Roy has a short fuse. He's right about that, and if we don't find a good paystreak soon, I'm afraid Roy's going to blow sky high.

December 20, 1898

I'll never get tired of watching the northern lights. The aurora borealis, Mr. Brennan calls them. The tiny bit of sunlight we get around noon is so pale we can hardly see anything, but once in a while the auroras flood the whole snow-white valley with light. Tonight the sky was draped with gold and green ribbons that rippled as though they were blowing in some magical wind.

December 25, 1898

A letter! Aunt Rachel says she's written four of them, but this is only the second one that's reached us. It arrived by dogsled on the Mounties' mail run from Lake Bennett to Dawson. Mr. Brennan picked it up for us when he mushed in to Dawson to buy a treat for Christmas dinner at the McGees'.

Tim hunched near the candle, writing in his journal. Aunt Rachel's questions about the northern lights and how they managed to keep from freezing to death reminded him of a few other details he'd meant to jot down. Not that there was anything too exciting to write about, stuck in the cabin these dark days.

"What's this all about, then?" The anger in Roy's voice brought Tim's head up with a snap. His brother came thudding down from his upper bunk brandishing Aunt Rachel's letter. "What have you been writing her? That we're destitute? Not able to take care of ourselves?"

"I just told her we were working the McGees' claim." The words came out too loudly. The minute Tim had read Aunt Rachel's closing words, he'd known, with a queasy twist of his stomach, that Roy would be furious. "At least you've found someone to keep you from starving," the letter ended. He could just hear his aunt's tart tone.

"You keep our business private from now on, hear?" Tim ducked away as Roy shook the crumpled letter in his face. "That's all she needs — proof I've failed, just like she always said I would. Never you mind writing to her anymore."

Suddenly Tim was fed up with Roy and his touchiness. "I'll write if I feel like it. She's the only kin we've got. Besides I *like* finding out what's going on at home."

"Then you should have *stayed* at home — you and that dog of yours. What good have you been?"

"Good enough to get you taken on here." Anger blazed through Tim. He couldn't stop himself. All the hurts from the past year made him shout, "And it was *my* money paid your way." The satisfaction of throwing those words at his brother was over in a flash.

Roy, looming over him, gritted his teeth. "What did you say?" One hand twisted Tim's shirt front, pulling him half out of the chair. Tim shrank away, his heart beating wildly as Roy raised the other hand, clenched it into a fist.

The suspended second of silence was shattered by the soft thump, thump of Ned's pipe against his palm. Both brothers turned, startled, as Ned got up from his chair and walked slowly past them to the stove to tap the dottle from his pipe into the fire.

Not a word was spoken, but Roy's fingers loosened and Tim felt himself slumping against the back of his chair. Roy would never hit him.

Would he? He watched as Roy slowly swung himself back up on his bunk. Then, with a shaking hand, Tim smoothed down the page of his journal and picked up his pencil.

The air had been tense with simmering anger ever since. Tim had spent the last few hours making as little noise as possible. He'd felt a prickle of alarm when Roy followed him outside to the bonfire he'd built under a tub of melting snow. But all Roy said was, "You'll need a hand lifting that down." And they'd worked in silence, hefting the sloshing tub into the cabin and ladling water into smaller containers.

They weren't expected at the McGees' until mid-afternoon, so after a noon meal of warmed-up beans and bannock, Tim got out their pack of cards. Ned was reading by lantern light, comfortable in his sock feet in the armchair he'd knocked together from sturdy branches. Roy seemed to have gone to sleep on his bunk.

Tim whistled under his breath as he picked the top card off the pile. Let it be five, five of clubs. He glanced at it quickly. Yes! Exactly what he needed. He slapped it down on the growing line of clubs. That let him move the six. And yes, under it the three of diamonds. And there was the seven of spades. Slap. Slap, slap. The lines were growing. He was going to win!

"Will you stop that infernal racket?" Roy leaped from the upper bunk and Tim hunched over his cards protectively. He wouldn't put it past Roy to send the cards flying to the four corners of the cabin.

Ned closed his book with a snap. "Steady on, Roy! The boy's just passing the time."

"I can't stand this sitting around any longer. I'm going out."

Tim kept still until Roy had finished raging around the cabin, snatching his coat from the hook, his boots from beside the door.

As long as Roy was outside helping to dig the shaft, he'd come in too tired to do anything but collapse on his bunk. But after a few hours crammed in the tiny cabin with Tim and Ned, Roy's mood soon turned sour. Still, Tim thought, you'd think Christmas coming would cheer him up. Even Mr. Brennan was looking forward to Christmas at the McGees' roadhouse.

Roy had himself bundled up at last. As he pulled the door open, frigid air swirled into the stuffy cabin. In less than a second he'd slammed it behind him, but Tim still shivered. Five miles to the roadhouse. Of course, he'd been out in worse — just this time last year, climbing the Chilkoot. Their snug cabin, "windproof thanks to your chinking," Ned had pointed out, was making him soft. These days he had to force himself out into the cold.

Tim looked at his game laid out neatly in rows, the cards shining slickly against the rough-cut lumber of the tabletop. Could he win? The cards he really needed were in the discard pile. Ned's rules said only the last discard could be used, and Tim wasn't ready yet for the jack of diamonds staring up at him. He sighed. Well, it had been exciting for a while. He swept up the cards and stacked them in a neat pile. Time to gather the things they were taking down to the McGees'.

High on the shelf where Ned kept the coarse gold, Tim had tucked his present for Flora — a handkerchief box made from one of Mr. Brennan's wooden cigar boxes. Ned had shown him how to carve a design on the top and Tim had spent hours on a spray of fireweed, carefully cutting around the petals so that each one stood out. "Darn good, for a first try," Ned had said.

Tim glanced over at Ned. "Thanks for sticking up for me."

"Cabin fever," Ned said around the stem of his pipe. He held a burning splint to the bowl and sucked until he was puffing smoke. "Happens all the time. Having three maybe helps. Heard about two fellas divided the cabin down the middle. Protected their territory like mad dogs."

Tim grinned and realized his cheek muscles were stiff from lack of smiling these long, dark days. Still, it wasn't just cabin fever. A blowup had been building for a long time. Maybe ever since the day they started out. He swallowed and forced himself to say out loud the suspicion he'd been trying to smother for months. "I guess it was a mistake, me coming here. I'm not much of a help to Roy. He'd do better without Pal and me." He didn't look up, afraid to see confirmation in Ned's eyes.

"Well now." Ned puffed at his pipe for a moment. "Maybe I see it a bit different. Problem's not you so much. It's that black dog on your brother's back."

Tim looked up. What was Ned talking about? What black dog?

"Something my old mother used to say when she saw envy and jealousy eating away at someone."

"Jealousy? You mean because we got here too late to stake a claim of our own?"

"Could be. But I see a fella feels everything he does falls flat — couldn't get a job back home, took a desperate chance coming here. Maybe that's gone bust, too."

"But he got us over the Chilkoot. He got us down the river."

"That's what we see. Wonder what he sees? Another thing — that's quite a debt he owes you. How'll he pay you back, happen there's nothing at the bottom of that shaft?"

"Is that what you think? There's nothing down there?"

"Mining's a gamble, son. No way *I* can predict what's down that hole. Now me, I've got a half-share of a ranch to go back to. Sure, a bag of gold'd make me happy. But if all I get's a grand adventure, I'm still happy."

"And without the bag of gold, Roy won't be happy?"

"Reckon it'll take more'n that."

"I don't understand."

Ned paused, then shrugged and plunged on. "Reckon he sees a younger brother coming along who's a little quicker on the uptake than he is. Look at it his way — the McGees no sooner clap eyes on you than they're offering you part of their claim, then Pat Brennan's buzzing around you like a honeybee around clover. Even the dog growls at Roy. There's old Roy slogging away and it's you has all the friends."

"But I never meant to . . ."

"You know that and I know that. Don't reckon Roy does, though." Ned shrugged. "I dare say he'll come 'round — should we all live long enough."

Tim caught Ned's wry smile and thought, If only Roy could be more like Ned. Life would be so much easier.

He looked down at the decorated box. "Roy isn't back yet. I — I was kind of hoping to get there a little early. To give Flora her present before everyone arrived."

"You go on ahead. I'll wait for Roy. Just stick to the trail we broke a few days back." Ned and Tim had mushed downriver to ice-fish. On the way back, they had a nice grayling to drop off at the roadhouse — a little change from bacon for Christmas dinner, Ned had said.

Tim felt elated. Ned always had the answer. He could give Flora her present and, a niggling little voice said, he wouldn't have to face Roy with these strange new thoughts buzzing around in his head. "Here, Pal. Let's get these boots on you."

To protect Pal's feet from ice shards on the trail, he'd cut four circles from a piece of soft leather. Pal didn't like the boots but Tim had used treats of cooked bacon to train him to leave them on. He tied each one firmly with a thong before shrugging into his heavy wool coat. As he wound Aunt Rachel's scarf of many colors around his neck, he thought, She'll be happy to know how useful this is. I'll tell her when I write back. He pulled the scarf up to cover his nose and cheeks, then pulled on padded canvas mitts over Aunt Rachel's woolen ones. And, he thought defiantly, I *am* going to write back.

"See you down there, then." Tim opened the door and the cold caught him sharply across the eyes, the only exposed bit of his face. Even breathing through the scarf, he felt the frigid air freeze his nose hairs. An hour to the roadhouse. And just enough twilight left to get him there.

Pal seemed pleased to be out. He set a brisk pace as they started down the trail. Tramping behind him, Tim felt the tensions of the day seep away. Christmas dinner. The thought cheered him. Christmas is no time to be glum and mopey, he decided. What had Flora told him? It was a tradition here for neighbors to pool their food and have a big celebration. His pack was weighted down with his own contribution, three cans of peaches.

It'll be great fun. If only Roy doesn't spoil it. Tim felt a twinge of apprehension. Roy's moods were so unpredictable. No, Ned's right, it's just that we've all been cooped up too long. But he couldn't push away the sick feeling that he was stuck — a thousand miles from home — with a brother who hated him.

A sharp bark from Pal startled Tim out of his thoughts. He stopped short. A ghostly fog encircled them like a gray shroud. He could barely see the canvas mitt at the end of his outstretched arm. Even Pal, just a few steps ahead, seemed to dissolve in the gloom.

"Heel, Pal!" Tim's voice was sharp with panic. Why hadn't he brought the lead? If he and Pal got separated . . . His heart began to thud. Mr. Brennan had warned him about these freezing fogs and how quickly they could form. He crouched down and hugged Pal. The dog's warmth and soft whimperings calmed him. Think, he commanded himself. The trail was packed hard and led straight to the roadhouse. Just put one foot in front of the other. That was easy enough. He stood, still a little shaky. "Heel," he said firmly to Pal, "heel!" and took courage from the dog pressed close to his side.

He wanted to hold out his hands to ward off obstacles but he knew it was his feet he had to think about. With a firm trail under him, he was fine. After a few hesitant steps, he felt his confidence returning. Concentrate on the feet, he kept telling himself.

It must be close now. How far had they gone before the fog came down? Ice from his breath rimmed his scarf. That took only a few minutes out in this cold. But now his fingers were tingling inside his bulky mitts and his feet felt heavy. Surely it would take more than half an hour to get that cold. They *must* be close. Slapping his mitts together to warm his hands, he stepped out confidently. Even in this blinding fog he should soon see lights from the roadhouse. Any minute now . . .

Suddenly Tim's foot twisted under him. He pitched forward and found himself floundering knee-high in snow. He was off the trail! Through the fog came Pal's frantic barking. He turned and stumbled toward the sound. The trail should be right here. But now he was wading in waist-high snow, his hands flailing in front of him. Where was Pal? The barking seemed so close. He pushed forward. The snow wasn't as deep now, but he kept stumbling on the uneven ground. All around him shapes loomed then faded like gray ghosts. Trees. Was he going farther away from the trail? He stopped, brushing at his eyes as though that would clear his sight. He took another step. His foot met nothing. He was falling.

* * *

The pain started in his fingertips — a dull throbbing ache that ran in jagged streaks up his arms. His eyelids felt like lead shutters. Struggling to open them took his mind off the ache in his hands. What had happened? His fingers — stiff as wood — were cold. Where were his mitts? He'd get frostbite! With a panicky start, Tim forced his eyes open. A blurry face

swam into focus. Ned! Tim realized he was lying down and Ned was holding his hands in a bucket of snow.

"Don't struggle now," Ned said in a soothing voice. "I'm just thawing your hands out slowly. This'll stop 'em from paining too much."

"Where am I?" The flickering light hurt his eyes. He had to close them again.

"Roy found you about ten minutes up the trail from the roadhouse. You'd hit your head against a whacking great rock."

Pat Brennan took up the tale. "That dog of yours come whining up to the door just as we're gettin' suited up to go look for you. Roy was out the door before the rest of us could work out what was happening. Him and the dog disappeared into the fog, so we had nothing to follow but his trail. Ned and me hadn't mushed very far before Roy come charging out of that fog like a steam engine, lugging you over his shoulder and the dog limping along at his side."

"Real heroes, your brother and that dog of yours," Ned put in.

"'Twas me knowed about putting your hands in snow. He was all for getting hot water. Worst thing you can do for frostbite. Not that you've got much of a case there. Still and all . . ."

The voice droned on but Tim wasn't listening anymore. One phrase kept repeating in his head: ". . . Roy come charging out of that fog . . . lugging you over his shoulder . . ." Tears rushed to Tim's eyes. He had to say something, to thank Roy. He pushed himself up on one elbow. The room swam before his eyes.

"Take it easy," he heard Ned say. He looked across the room and there was Roy scraping cornmush and pork scraps into a dish while Pal sat on his haunches watching him intently. Just then Roy looked over and caught Tim's eye. His thin, dark face lit with a half smile and Tim felt warmth flood through him.

He lay down again and must have fallen asleep. A clinking sound woke him. He opened his eyes and this time the room didn't spin. Almost close enough for him to reach out and touch her, Flora was setting the table, plunking down the knife, fork, cup and plate each guest had been asked to bring.

Tim blinked as he took in the rest of his surroundings. The roadhouse had been transformed. Evergreen boughs tied with bright red bows framed its two front windows. The rough plank table was covered with a white cloth, and for a centerpiece someone had made flowers from the silver foil that tea was packed in. Tim counted — Ned, Roy, Mr. Brennan, two men he didn't know very well from claims closer to the roadhouse, Flora, Mrs. McGee and himself — eight for dinner.

From the oven came the smell of wild fowl roasting, and on top of the stove their grayling poached in a pan of water. Tim's mouth watered as he breathed in the succulent smells. Then a thought struck him. He struggled to sit up. "My pack. Where's my pack?"

Ned shook his head. "Sorry, son. No pack when Roy and Pal brought you in."

Tim turned to Flora in dismay. "Your present. It's in my pack."

"Don't worry," Flora said. "Maybe we'll find it when the fog lifts. Or," her smile was teasing, "you can just give this present back to me."

She handed Tim a flat package wrapped in a white handkerchief. Inside were ten sheets of stiff brown paper. Barely visible wrinkles showed how carefully she had smoothed out the butcher's paper from some long-ago purchase. Tim looked up in surprise.

"That's so you can write the story of winter in the diggings for the Klondike Nugget. I knew you wouldn't want to tear pages out of your journal. When I see your story printed in the newspaper — that'll be my present."

The party swirled around him. Pat Brennan, looking a little self-conscious, produced a mouth organ and began to play softly. Then Flora's voice, high and sweet, filled the room. "Silent night, holy night. All is calm, all is bright . . ."

How many times had they sung that at home standing around a shining tree, presents piled high beneath? Not many presents this year — not compared to when their parents were alive. He looked over to where Roy sat smiling as he joined with the others in the old familiar carol. Who needed gifts wrapped in colored paper?

Tim took a deep breath to join in the singing. He and Roy were buddies again. Even better, they were brothers.

CABIN LIFE

December 30, 1898

The moon is so bright tonight I had no trouble finding my way to the woodpile to get firewood. Everything feels topsy-turvy now. The days are dark but the nights are often lit up either by moonlight or the northern lights. And now that Ned's watch has stopped, we have no notion of what time it is. If it was summer the sun would give us a clue, but now only our stomachs grumbling tell us when it's mealtime.

Winter seemed long and dreary to the miners. Their cabins were small, 3.5 m (12 ft.) by 4.25 m (14 ft.) with barely 2.5 m (8 ft.) of headroom under the highest point of the roof. The walls were made of logs and the roof poles were covered in a deep layer of earth. To conserve heat, door and window openings were small. Glass was difficult to come by, so often a row of bottles was fitted into the window opening. At least two and sometimes four men shared this small space with bunks, food supplies and a wood-burning Yukon stove.

Life in such cramped quarters could be unpleasant. Mice, attracted by food and warmth, were bad enough, but no one could tolerate for long the fleas and lice that infested the bedrolls. Every so often, bedrolls were thrown outdoors to freeze out the itchy pests.

And then there was the smell. When the men came in from digging the shaft, they hung sweat-soaked clothes around the cabin to dry. These smells, mixed with the odor of seldom-washed bodies, created a pungent atmosphere in the overheated cabin.

As winter days grew shorter, life in the cabin became tedious. Chores were the only distraction. Most important was keeping a large supply of firewood piled just outside the door, not only to thaw the frozen muck in the shaft, but also to keep the fire going inside.

KEEPING WARM

By mid-October snow was falling. It was time to make preparations for the cold weather soon to come. Tim had stuffed moss mixed with mud into the chinks between the logs to stop drafts. Snow settling on the roof added more insulation to the earth already piled there. And Roy and Tim shoveled more snow up against the walls.

Draft-free cabins could be kept remarkably warm just from the heat of their Yukon stoves. Even so, as the temperature dropped, frost appeared on the inside of the bottle window, made white dots out of nail heads and outlined the door. The wooden walls cracked loudly as they contracted in the cold. On the rare occasions when clothes were washed, they froze solid on the outside line and had to be draped around the cabin to finish drying.

Some miners liked to keep track of the deepening cold. A Klondike thermometer consisted of four tins sitting on an outside shelf. The first was filled with mercury, the second with whiskey, next kerosene, then a patented painkiller. Mercury solidified at -40°C (-40°F), whiskey at -48° C (-55°F), kerosene at -51°C (-60°F) and the patented painkiller at too low a temperature to measure. One miner commented that a man would start on a journey happily if the mercury had solidified, hesitantly at whiskey and reluctantly at kerosene. He would refuse to leave the cabin when the painkiller froze.

Klondike Solitaire

To relieve the monotony of winter life and prevent cabin fever, stampeders played endless games of a type of solitaire called Klondike. Here's how to play it.

You'll need:
a deck of playing cards

1. Shuffle the deck. Starting at the left, deal a row of seven cards, face down.

2. Deal a second row of six cards face down, starting with the second card from the left. Continue dealing cards, starting one card farther in each time until the seventh pile has seven cards.

3. Turn the top card of each pile face up. The remaining 24 cards are the stockpile. Turn them face down.

4. Look at the face-up cards. Red cards (hearts and diamonds) can be moved onto black cards (clubs and spades) in descending order. For example, a black 3 can be moved onto a red 4. When a card is moved from a pile, turn the one underneath face up.

5. Try to move cards onto other piles as described in 4 above. When there are no more opportunities to move cards from these piles, turn the first card in your stockpile face up. If it can't be played, put it face up in a discard pile and turn up another card from the stockpile. You can go through the stockpile only once.

130

6. As aces appear, place them above your row of cards. Once an ace has been moved up, you can build on it. For example, if the ace of diamonds has been moved up, you can put the 2 of diamonds on top of it, followed by the 3 of diamonds, the 4 of diamonds and so on. Always watch for cards that you can add to the aces.

7. As you play, watch to see if the top card of the discard pile can be played. Only the top card can be used.

8. If a pile is eliminated, the space can be filled only by a king.

9. You win if you manage to complete an ascending sequence of cards on each of the four aces.

CABIN FEVER

Long, dark days and cramped cabins were the undoing of many a partnership up and down the Klondike. By midwinter even the few hours of twilight had disappeared and darkness lasted around the clock. Miners had nothing to do but sit and stare at each other over the flickering light of a candle. They often lost track of time. Was it day or night? Time for breakfast or time for bed?

After days of this, every tic and quirk of a cabin mate could irritate. Tensions built and built until something as minor as one partner clearing his throat made the other snap. Stories were told of miners who wouldn't talk to each other all winter or of one partner who drew a line down the center of the cabin and refused to let the other cross. One man moved out of the cabin and lived in a tent; another waited until his partner had gone to town, then set fire to the cabin. He later insisted that it was only his half he'd planned to burn down.

WINTER WORK

January 30, 1899

What an eerie sight! For all the world as if swarms of giant fireflies are flickering up and down the valley. But it's just the fires set at every claim to thaw another few inches of muck.

Tim and his partners were lucky. The hard work of digging out gold-bearing gravel had been started by Mr. McGee. But as soon as they had washed the gold out of his dump (pile of gravel) they had to start digging for themselves.

They marked off a space about 2 m (6 ft.) square and began to shovel. After the first few centimeters (inches), they hit frozen muck. Before they could dig any farther down, they had to set fires on the surface to thaw the

The dumps grew higher and higher as the miners worked through the long winter.

muck. When they got too deep to throw dirt out of the shaft, they rigged up a winch to hoist it by the bucketful.

The digging continued until they reached bedrock. Any gold in the gravel would have been washed down to this shelf of solid rock. If they found a reasonable amount of gold, they would start to drift (tunnel) to follow the paystreak (gravel containing enough gold to make it worth the hard work of digging out). Gravel taken from the paystreak is called paydirt. It is piled above ground in the dump to wait for spring cleanup.

Every so often they would wash some of the paydirt to test for gold and be sure they were drifting in the right direction. If they found little gold, they would abandon that shaft and start another. Finding gold was a gamble and miners had to keep taking chances.

CLEANING THE GOLD

Once they had the gold-bearing dirt, they had to pan the gold out and clean it. First, it was poured into a shallow pan and set over a hot fire. As the gold "roasted" it was turned over and over with a small spoon-shaped instrument until it was as dry as powder. Roasting frees the gold dust by burning off sulfur and arsenic, which often combine with gold to make a sulfide. Although the miner roasted whenever he had gold to clean, by far the greatest amount was roasted after spring cleanup.

The roasted gold was scooped into a triangular metal dish called a blower. The miner carefully blew across the dish to clear out any particles of sand and earth, then tipped the clean gold into a container. Empty tins or jam jars were often used to store gold. For the trip into town, the gold was poured into canvas or leather pokes.

HEART'S DESIRE

February 10, 1899

The dumps get taller week by week. Ours, too. The day we hit bedrock I took a candle down the shaft and pried nuggets out of the cracks in the rock. Not as much gold as Ned was hoping for, but gold all the same. Now he and Roy are drifting in the hope of finding the paystreak.

February 15, 1899

Every day we pan gravel from the shaft to test for gold. For a while we were getting enough to keep Ned and Roy tunneling, but for three days now there's been hardly a trace of color in the pan. First time I've seen Ned discouraged, and Roy's worrying about money again. If we don't find at least a little gold, how'll we get home?

February 20, 1899

We spent the day at the roadhouse so Ned could talk things over with Mrs. McGee. They made the big decision — we're to start a new shaft. So much hope and work went into this one. Now, nothing. Flora was so upset she'd hardly talk to me.

February 25, 1899

Started the new shaft today — 6 feet across. I'm helping Ned and Roy dig through the thawed gravel. Slow work. In this cold, our fires thaw only 6 to 8 inches a time.

March 10, 1899

Five feet down and still nothing but gravel. Mining's a gamble, Ned keeps saying. Well, we're betting a hard winter's work that we'll find gold when we hit bedrock. Reminds me of Jake's kind of gambling. Bet he's snug and warm somewhere in Dawson. No way he'd be freezing out on a claim like us. So who's the real gambler?

March 23, 1899

My hand is shaking so much I can hardly write. Today, 15 feet down, we hit bedrock. Ned came up the ladder carrying a panful of gravel and we all went into the cabin to test it. My throat was too dry to swallow — and I sure couldn't bear to look at Roy. Even Ned was holding his breath as he swirled the pan in the tub of water. Roy and I just stared as the mud and gravel washed out of the pan. Finally a dull gleam. Ned gave a last swirl and a gold tail flared out of the black sand like fireworks in the night sky. A $10 pan! Ned's voice was all croaky as he said it. We've done it — we've struck it rich at last! The three of us danced around that pan of gold as if we were demented. Maybe we were. If so, it's a grand feeling.

A motley collection, that's for sure, Tim thought, surveying the rows of mismatched jam jars and tobacco tins lined up on the shelf above the table. But what a beautiful sight! Every last one full of gold. He grinned to himself, alone in the cabin with their treasure.

Ned and Roy were outside washing gravel for all they were worth. The spring runoff wouldn't last much longer and even though they had dammed up a few ponds to collect water for later, Ned said the washing they did now was what counted most.

Tim ladled a scoopful of gold dust from the roasting pan and blew across it. Fine sand rose into the air, settling onto the table and nearby shelves. As he tipped the cleaned gold dust into an empty tin, Tim felt his heart leap. If the paystreak stays this rich — who knows? We might end up like Big Alex McDonald, the King of the Klondike. It was said he handed out nuggets to anyone passing by.

Pal was draped across the threshold snoozing. Suddenly he opened one eye and gave a small bark. Then he was on his feet, tail wagging.

"What is it, boy?" But Pal had trotted off without a backward glance. Tim dumped the rest of the roasted gold into the tin. He was stashing it on the shelf when Flora appeared in the doorway.

Without saying a word, she put her basket on the table and lifted out some small canvas bags. Pokes — for carrying the gold into Dawson, she'd said the first time she brought some. Handier than tins and safer than jars.

Tim frowned. Flora usually started chattering the minute she arrived. What was going on?

Might as well break the ice. "How's your mother?"

"Still coughing."

Florence McGee had them all worried. She'd had to give up visiting the claim in the cold weather, and even now she often had to sit for minutes

after she made the climb, coughing like she was going to turn inside out.

"Sorry to hear that." Not much else he could say. The look on Flora's face was making him fidgety. "Let's go out. I've been cooped up cleaning gold since breakfast."

Flora stayed where she was, smoothing and resmoothing her stack of pokes. "I came to tell you . . . That is, Mother . . ." She paused, then blurted out, "The Haggartys have been down talking to us."

"So?" But just the name struck alarm bells. Mr. Brennan was always railing on about "them Haggartys."

"They're talking to owners up and down the creek. Trying to buy claims." She paused. "They've offered for ours — too good an offer to refuse."

Tim felt as though Flora had hit him in the chest with a shovel. "Sell the claim? But what about all the gold we're washing out of it?"

"Ned says the paystreak's running out."

Sure, Tim acknowledged to himself, Ned had been disappointed with the last gravel they'd dug out. "But once spring runoff's over, Ned said we'd dig another shaft. Anyway, why would the Haggartys want it if there's no gold left?"

"They want to bring in big machines. Go after the gold left in the tailings, they say."

Tim's mouth went dry. He could hardly bring himself to ask, "What's your mother going to do?"

Flora's averted eyes told him. Mrs. McGee wasn't well and Flora had always wanted to leave. That was what her silence was all about. Just when everything was going so well. It wasn't fair! Tim turned away, reaching for the pan of roasted gold as the cold truth hit him. It was the McGees' claim after all. He and Roy had no say in what happened to it.

"Coming?" She was halfway out the door.

Tim shook his head and picked up the blower. What the heck! Keep cleaning the gold — just like he was hired help. Which is probably how she thinks of me, he reflected bitterly.

He had finished cleaning all the gold in the pan when Roy stuck his head through the doorway.

"Where's dinner? Thought you were in here cooking."

Yep, hired help, that's me, Tim thought, and kept right on pouring the cleaned gold into a jam jar.

Roy sighed and sat down on the doorstep. "What's up?"

"You tell me. You were the one talking to Mrs. McGee."

Roy rubbed one hand over his stubbly chin. "Listen, Tim, I haven't time for this right now. We're still finishing up for the day. You talked to Flora. You know what's going on. We'll discuss it later, but let's get on with the grub, eh?"

Tim nodded, disappointment rising sourly in his throat. Roy's words confirmed what he was hoping against hope wasn't true. Just when they'd struck it rich. Just when they'd finally made it.

He had a pot of beans heating on the stove and sourdough biscuits warming in the oven when he heard Ned and Roy splashing in the washing-up bucket outside the door.

"Time to tote 'er all into Dawson," Ned was saying. "Find out for sure how much we have."

Ned and Roy had no sooner sat down than they were stuffing forkfuls of beans into their mouths. Tim knew not to ask questions until they had satisfied the ravenous hunger that came from hours of slogging work.

Finally, Ned broke a biscuit in half and ran it around his plate, mopping up the last of the gravy. "Well, son, guess you know what Mrs. McGee had to say."

Tim nodded. "She's going to sell the claim." Then he blurted out an idea that had hit him in the middle of mixing up biscuits. "But I don't see why she has to sell to the Haggartys. Why don't *we* buy the McGees out? The three of us. Our share of the gold would be enough for that."

Roy kept shoveling beans into his mouth, but Ned stopped chewing and gave Tim a thoughtful look. "You figure to work here through another season?"

"You said yourself if one shaft plays out, you dig another. If this one was so rich, there must be more gold down there — just waiting for us."

"How much gold you figure you need?"

"For what?"

"For whatever it is you want to do. The McGees figure they have enough now to set them up Outside. Not rich, but comfortable. How much do you want?"

Tim looked away from Ned's steady gaze. How much gold *did* he want? Enough to impress Aunt Rachel? Enough to be a King of the Klondike? All he could do was shrug.

"Let's face it, son. This claim hasn't done badly by us. Maybe it's time to move on. Nice biscuits," he ended, stuffing a whole one into his mouth.

Later, washing dishes by the door of the cabin, Tim brooded on the unfairness, the miserable unfairness of it all. Just when they had it right in their hands. Their wildest dreams about to be fulfilled — then gone, just like that. He dumped the tin plates into the washing-up pan.

Roy sat nearby puffing on a pipe to keep the mosquitoes at bay. "Don't you care?" Tim burst out at him. "You wanted so badly to get here. Don't you care that we're finished?"

Roy brushed a cloud of mosquitoes off his bare forearm and slowly rolled down his sleeves. "You want to know what I felt when Mrs. McGee told us about the Haggartys?" he started slowly. "Relief. That's what." He looked Tim right in the eye. "Sure, I was desperate to get here — and I know it's thanks to you we had the chance."

Tim was amazed. Roy! Saying thank you? He felt such a warm glow spreading through him he almost missed Roy's next question.

"You want to spend the rest of your life here, shoveling a ton of gravel for every ounce of gold? Turn into a broken-down old curmudgeon like Pat Brennan? You can have it. Not me. That gold? I see it as a grubstake. For back home. I aim to set up as a storekeeper, not rot here as a gravel grubber."

Pal padded over and rested his nose on Roy's knee. Roy rubbed at a spot between Pal's ears and Tim watched resentfully as Pal's eyes closed in contentment. Even my dog's deserted me, he thought.

Two days later, they set off at dawn to backpack the gold to the roadhouse. Mrs. McGee had made arrangements for the mule train to take it the rest of the way into Dawson. And sure enough, when they got within sight of the roadhouse, there were the mules, waiting for them.

"I'm sorry it's worked out this way," Flora said. They were walking down the trail at the end of a long procession — the mules and their drivers, Mrs. McGee sidesaddle on one of the mules, then Roy and Ned.

Tim just shrugged. He did mind giving up. But it wasn't just the gold he regretted. Where else would he ever meet characters like Ned or Jake or Mr. Brennan? And then there was Flora. Without her, would he have pushed himself to get on with his writing? Tucked inside his shirt, on four of the brown sheets of paper she had given him for Christmas, was the story he'd worked on all winter — "Climbing the Chilkoot with a Real Pal," he'd called it.

Long before they reached Dawson, they heard the pounding of hammers. Of course, they knew about the big fire in April. Building after building had collapsed in ashes until finally the Mounties had blown some up to make a fire gap — to stop the wild flames from devouring the entire town. "Fire so hot a river of molten gold ran out of the Bank of North America vault," Pat Brennan had reported.

Tim was expecting a burned-out shell of a town, but as he trailed across the bridge behind the pack mules, he was amazed to see new buildings everywhere. The town seemed bigger, more solid and . . . would you look at that! Marching down the street a line of poles strung with electric wires. "Not taking any more chances on overturned lamps, I see," Ned remarked dryly.

They headed for the big sign "Gold Dust Bought Here." The bank was little more than a shack with a plank counter, but it was doing a roaring business. Miners were lined up out the door and down the street. All were anxious to cash in on their long winter's work now that spring cleanup had released the gold.

It took two hours of inching their way up the line to get inside the small, dark room. They'd each taken turns holding a place in line while the others roamed the town. But Tim and Flora were standing right there when Roy and Ned heaved their sacks of gold onto the big scales.

As the clerks poured and weighed, poured and weighed, Tim watched the little group he'd come to think of as his family. Their thoughts were written right on their faces. Mrs. McGee looked years younger, relief smoothing the care from her forehead. For Flora, each weight added to the pan was another mile chugged off on the train trip across the continent to her new life in Toronto. And Roy — Roy was already behind the counter of his grocery store, a clean apron just tied on, serving his first customer. Ned wasn't quite so easy to read. What had he said? *If I take a bag of gold home, I'm happy.* Well, he had his bag of gold and then some. And by his face, he was quietly happy.

They split the gold right there in the bank. Mrs. McGee worked out each person's share and instructed the clerks how to fill out the bank drafts.

It seemed odd, Tim thought, staring at "Tim Olsen" and "$10 000" scratched in ink on the printed document — nearly two years of his life reduced to a piece of paper. Had he really expected to lug a suitcase full of gold home to Aunt Rachel? Well, at least he had two nuggets to show her — thanks to Mr. Brennan.

After that, everyone went in different directions. Roy and Ned headed for a barber to have a hot bath and a haircut. "Won't know us when you see us," Ned joked. Flora and Mrs. McGee had an appointment with someone interested in buying the roadhouse.

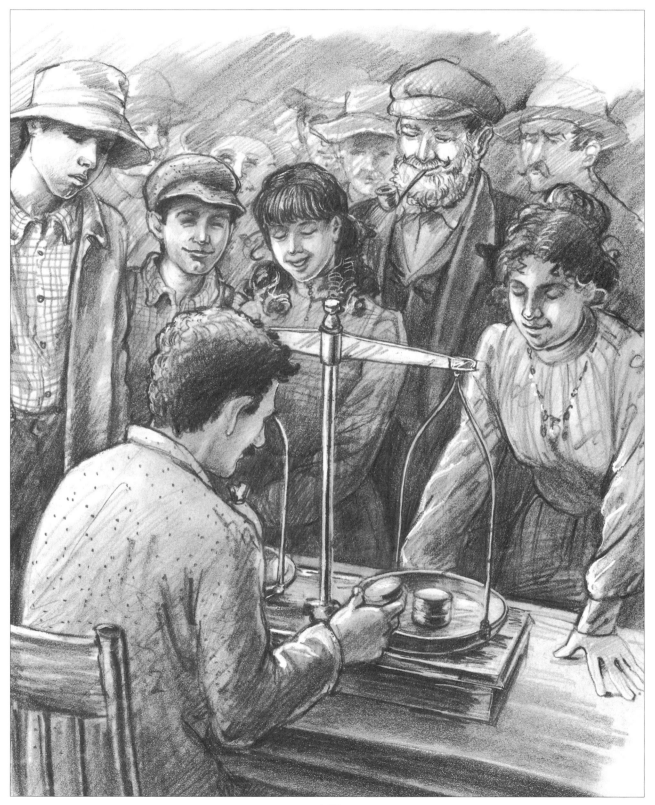

"Don't forget," Mrs. McGee reminded them. "The Fairview, in an hour. We'll have the best meal they have to offer. To celebrate."

Tim watched them all head away. The flat package tucked inside his shirt was sticky with sweat after the hike into town, but he left it there. It would be just like Flora to suddenly pop up in front of him and demand to know what it was and where he was going. When everyone had finally disappeared into the milling crowds, Tim wrapped Pal's lead several times around his hand, took a deep breath and stepped down off the boardwalk.

Once across the street, standing in front of the Klondike Nugget, he felt conspicuous. Did everyone brushing past know why he was there? He pretended to study the news board beside the front door. "President Sends Reinforcements to Philippines to Put Down Rebellion," screamed the headline. Imagine sending in that story. A foreign correspondent. What would it take to be a foreign correspondent? Well, what the heck. I gambled on the gold rush and that paid off. Why not try another gamble?

Tim pushed open the door. The chunk, chunk of a handpress made the rough plank floor shudder under his feet. He breathed in to calm his thudding heart, then coughed as cigar smoke and the smell of ink caught in his throat.

"Be right with you."

The man running the machine had deep paper cuffs protecting his shirt and a green visor over his eyes. He turned toward Tim and his brows snapped together. "Oh — a kid. Thought you were a customer."

"My . . . my name's Tim Olsen, sir. I've written . . . that is . . . brought you . . ." His throat was so dry he could barely croak, ". . . a story." Tim fumbled the package out of his shirt and thrust it at the man — four of Flora's neatly ironed sheets of butcher's paper covered in his best handwriting.

With an impatient sigh, the man snatched it and ran a quick eye down the first page. Tim had just steeled himself to grab it back and flee when the man drew up a stool, perched himself on it and began again, reading slowly.

The sound of a page turning rasped on Tim's nerves. The occasional "hmm" made him start. He hates it, Tim decided, trying to make sense of the low mutterings that continued page after page.

"Well, kid, you've got a lot to learn. The hook needs more punch and your climax could stand a bit of work." A sick feeling started in the pit of Tim's stomach. He should have known. "But . . . I guess I can use it."

What? Had he heard right?

"With a bit of tweaking we can turn it into a crackerjack human interest story."

"Thank you, sir. Thank you," Tim finally managed to say. Then, in a great rush, "I've got five notebooks full of the same sort of material. I could write more for you."

"Hold on, son, don't get carried away. You *do* have a nice, fresh approach. And I could use the odd human interest story — miners eaten by bears, hikers frozen to death — that kind of stuff."

"I . . . I . . ."

"Nothing sensational. Just nice human interest stories. Oh, by the way, we pay five dollars for every one we use."

Tim stumbled out of the office. Five dollars a story! I could earn a living doing this! Once we get back to Seattle, I could be off . . . anywhere. Foreign Correspondent Tim Olsen, reporting from . . .

"We've done it!" Flora pranced up just as he got his trembling knees under control. "We've bought our tickets. For a month from today. Steamer to Lake Bennett, then the new train out to Skagway, then —" She broke off to stare at him and then at the sign behind him.

"Tim Olsen! Were you just in there?"

Tim couldn't stop a grin from splitting his face.

"You did it? You actually did it! What happened?"

"Five dollars he's going to pay me for this one. And five dollars more for every story he likes."

Flora grabbed both his hands and danced him in wild circles down Dawson's dusty main street. The crowds parted to flow around them and Pal yipped at their heels with excitement. Finally, out of breath, she stopped whirling and they both staggered over to the raised boardwalk and flopped down. "Who would have believed it? What wonderful luck we've all had!"

Luck? Tim thought, still trying to catch his breath. Was that all it was? Just a throw of the dice? Then what about all that hard work — keeping at it, day after freezing day? Surely it was putting one foot in front of the other and getting the job done that had made the difference.

"Mother will be waiting," Flora said, snapping him out of his musings. She stood up and smoothed down her skirts, then paused. "You know," she said slowly, "in a month we'll all be on our way out of Dawson, all our lives changed forever. We might never see one another again."

Tim nodded. "Toronto to Seattle. A whole continent apart."

"Tell you what. I'll watch for your stories in the newspapers."

"And I'll watch for your name — in the concert halls."

Flora blushed and shrugged. "Who knows?" For once, she looked shy, almost uncertain. "But at least I'm going to get a chance to try."

She slipped her arm through Tim's and together they walked along the plank boardwalk toward the Fairview Hotel. A chance, Tim thought. Roy's right. That's what this year has given us. A chance to try. And what more could anyone ask?

THE MYTHOLOGIZERS

The story of the Klondike Gold Rush was one of extremes. A harsh land, a journey of epic proportions to reach it, desperately poor men becoming Klondike Kings, only to throw away every penny — these ingredients would fire any imagination. And so the tall tales started. Miners huddled around stoves over the long winters told one another stories of impossible journeys endured, gruesome discoveries made as the snow melted, heroic rescues and dastardly deeds. These tales, with their larger-than-life characters, ignited the imaginations of two writers in particular. Out of the pain and hardship and determination of real heroes, they spun stories that grew into legends — stories that became, for future generations, the essence of the Klondike Gold Rush.

JACK LONDON

As a boy, Jack London spent little time in school. Instead he grew up around the docks in San Francisco and learned many tough lessons about the everyday world. At 17, he signed on to a sealing vessel bound for the Siberian coast. By 21, he was part of the rush to the Klondike.

With thousands of other stampeders, London climbed Chilkoot Pass, built a boat, sailed down the Yukon River to Dawson and tried prospecting. The hard work was too much for him, but he had fallen in love with the rugged land. Even though he took the first steamer out when the ice broke up in June 1898, his writer's imagination had soaked up vivid impressions of the North and stories of the hard life on the claims.

Back in civilization, he began writing magazine stories about the North. In 1903 he produced the story that for many summed up the gold rush experience. *The Call of the Wild* follows the adventures of Buck, a magnificent dog kidnapped in California and taken north to work as a sled dog in the Yukon. In this story and a companion story, *White Fang*, London shows how the struggle for survival can turn men into monsters. For many readers, these stories became the Klondike adventures they were not able to experience in person.

ROBERT SERVICE

There are strange things done in the midnight sun
By the men who moil for gold;
The Arctic trails have their secret tales
That would make your blood run cold.

— The Cremation of Sam McGee

The man who wrote these often-quoted lines about the gold rush was nowhere near the Yukon the year thousands were toiling over Chilkoot Pass. Twenty-year-old Robert Service had left England in 1894 looking for adventure. By 1897, when stampeders were rushing north, he was wandering aimlessly through Mexico and California. At the age of 29, while in British Columbia, he tired of the wandering life and became a clerk with the Canadian Bank of Commerce. A transfer to Whitehorse in 1904 introduced him to the wild and wonderful tales of the gold rush, by then long over. Inspired, Service began turning the stories into ballads and soon had written enough for a book.

Songs of a Sourdough, published in 1907, celebrated many aspects of northern life, but two stories in particular helped create the myth of the gold rush. *The Cremation of Sam McGee* and *The Shooting of Dan McGrew* have come to represent the very essence of gold rush life for later generations.

By the time Service first saw Dawson, his ballads of Klondike days were being recited all over the continent. Did it bother him that he didn't get the details quite right? *The Shooting of Dan McGrew*, for example, could never have happened in the real Dawson. The Mounties kept such a tight check on handguns that not one murder occurred that gold rush year.

Service may have exaggerated the events of the gold rush to make a good story, but he certainly understood how people could both love and hate the experience. About that ambivalent feeling, he wrote:

There's gold and it's haunting and haunting,
It's luring me on as of old;
Yet it isn't the gold that I'm wanting
So much as just finding the gold.

— The Spell of the Yukon

WINNERS AND LOSERS

Numbers were hard to keep track of during the big gold rush of 1897 to 1899. Rough estimates say 100 000 people started out for the Yukon once news of the great gold strike hit the headlines. About 30 000 made it all the way to Dawson. Almost none of them struck it rich. The real winners were the few hundred seasoned miners already in the North when George Carmack staked his claim on Bonanza Creek. They found the richest creeks, and a few of them actually managed to hold on to their money and live their lives out in comfort.

Among the real winners were Clarence and Ethel Berry. They were on the deck of the SS *Portland* that historic August day in 1897 when it pulled into Seattle. Dressed in rags though they were, at their feet lay a bedroll holding $100 000 in gold. And that was just the start of their fortune.

Clarence and Ethel were childhood sweethearts who had grown up on farms in central California. In the fall of 1895, when Clarence returned from his first trip to the Yukon, 23-year-old Ethel decided she'd had enough of waiting. If Clarence was going north again, she was going with him. They married in March 1896 and by June were living near Forty Mile Creek, which empties into the Yukon downstream from the Klondike River. To earn money for a grubstake, Clarence tended bar in the saloon. That was how he happened to be one of the first to hear George Carmack's big news about Bonanza Creek. The Berrys rushed right off and staked a claim on nearby Eldorado Creek. It turned out to be one of the most valuable claims in the Klondike.

With Ethel keeping house and Clarence working every minute of the long northern days, they soon had a fortune in nuggets and coarse gold neatly stored in jam jars. The Berrys' claim was so rich that Ethel later told reporters she could pick nuggets out of the dump like raisins out of a pudding. Altogether they took more than $1.5 million worth of gold out of their various claims before they retired to California, where wise investments kept their fortune growing.

Not every story worked out as happily as the Berrys'. Many of the winners eventually became losers. Big Alex McDonald, a day laborer from Nova Scotia, had worked for 14 years in the silver mines of Colorado when he decided to try his luck in the North. In 1897 he arrived in the Yukon to find that Bonanza Creek and Eldorado Creek were completely staked. But some of the stakeholders, nervous about the gold prospects of the untried creeks, were anxious to sell out. For a sack of flour and a side of bacon, Alex McDonald bought Claim #30 on Eldorado, the richest placer creek in the world. Its paystreak was so rich that $5000 was panned from it in a single day.

McDonald could have lived well on the output of that one claim alone, but he craved property. With money from #30 Eldorado, he started buying up claims and part claims on Bonanza and Eldorado Creeks, paying other men to work them. So rich were the claims that at cleanup time he had his own 15-mule train laden with gold that traveled constantly between the diggings and Dawson.

In Dawson, where Big Alex was called King of the Klondike, he often passed around a box of nuggets as if they were chocolates. Big Alex looked on gold as trash. Only property counted.

As the gold in his Bonanza and Eldorado claims ran out, he began buying claims recklessly. All his new claims proved worthless. By the end of his life, the King of the Klondike was a pauper, living alone in a small cabin on Clearwater Creek, still prospecting in the hope of finding another Eldorado.

SENDING THE GOLD OUTSIDE

In 1897 ragged, gumboot miners had dragged their gold by the suitcaseful all the way to Seattle or San Francisco. Only there could they find an assay office to test and value their gold. Only then did they know just how rich they were. But once the gold rush was in full swing, banks and government agencies were only too happy to help transport the gold.

In 1898 the Canadian Bank of Commerce sent clerks over Chilkoot Pass and down the Yukon River with all the equipment needed to assay gold. To pay for the gold, they carried with them bank draft forms for anyone headed Outside, and $1 million in paper money for miners who wanted cash. The word "Dawson" was stamped on the banknotes in case they went astray.

In Dawson the bank clerks set up shop in a tent. Their only equipment was a large set of scales and a ledger book to record transactions. Banknotes were stacked on the counter and sacks of gold were packed into tin-lined wooden boxes. Thanks to the North-West Mounted Police, few thought to steal the gold and no one succeeded.

The gold was transported by steamer to St. Michael's at the mouth of the Yukon River, then down the coast to Victoria, British Columbia. To keep it safe, escorts from the Yukon Field Force armed with Winchester rifles went with it. During the three years the gold rush lasted, they delivered millions of dollars in gold dust and ingots safely to Victoria's banks.

Gold, packed in long pokes made of caribou hide, is guarded by soldiers of the Yukon Field Force. These men were sent north to help the NWMP protect the territory.

THE END OF THE RUSH

Poor man's gold, as placer gold was often called, was all panned out by 1900. The nuggets and coarse gold that could be easily washed out of the gravel were on their way south to the bank vaults. But the Klondike still had gold for those who knew how to find it. The Haggartys were buying up claims because they knew the ground was still laced with gold dust missed by the inefficient methods of gumboot miners.

By the fall of 1899 a railway was running from Skagway through White Pass to Whitehorse. This meant large machines called dredges could be brought in to do the work of many men. A dredge scoops up gravel in buckets on a conveyer belt and runs it through a stream of water. Operated by only a few men, it can do the work of hundreds, processing many tonnes (tons) of gravel a day. Using dredges, mining companies recovered millions of dollars worth of gold left behind by the gumboot miners. In the three years the gold rush lasted, the banks sent just under $50 million worth of gold to the mints. In the next 50 years, mining companies processed $500 million worth of gold.

THE END OF THE DREAM

August 5, 1899

What a piece of news! Mr. Brennan's sold out to the Haggartys. "Made them pay, too, the crooks," he cackled when he came to tell us. Now he's talking about Alaska — a place downriver called Nome. He heard tell there's so much gold you can make a fortune just by panning the beach sand. Ned is skeptical. "It's easy to hit the mother lode of rumors," he says. "Gold country's full of rumors."

The Dawson that rose from the ashes of the fire of April 26, 1899, had a shinier face than the old town of log cabins and tents. The city council put in sewers to drain the streets, electricity to prevent another fire from carelessly handled candles and a telephone system. Some buildings even had steam heating and running water. All the conveniences of southern cities and then some could be found in the new Dawson.

But it was too late. The crowds still drifting from hotel to dance hall to gambling saloon knew the creeks were mined out. Only machines could get the gold that was left. It had been a grand adventure but now it was time to go home.

Or was it? Rumors came floating upriver to Dawson from the mouth of the Yukon. Gold! A buzz started among the idlers on the streets of Dawson. Gold in Alaska. And then came confirmation from an old prospector — he was panning gold from the sand on the beaches!

No mountains to cross. No frozen muck to dig through. Gold from the sands, just there for the picking.

Dawson went mad. By mid-August, every steamer heading downstream was crowded "like straphangers on a train," one man complained. And it was all true. There *was* gold in the sandy beach that stretched in front of the tiny community of Nome. But as the stampeders soon discovered, there was not nearly as much of it as in the Yukon. And just as in the Klondike rush, those first on the scene were the lucky ones.

Gradually gold fever died. Many thousands returned home poorer than they set out. But few regretted their end-of-century madness. It had been a great adventure — a story to tell for the rest of their lives.

GLOSSARY

bedrock—a layer of unbroken, solid rock beneath soil and gravel

bedroll—a portable roll of blankets usually used for sleeping outdoors

cache—a supply of food and equipment stored beside the trail while the next load was being fetched

claim — land that a miner "claimed" by driving in stakes to mark each corner, then registered in a claims office

cornmeal — coarsely ground corn used to make biscuits, bread and pancakes

creek bed — the bottom of a small stream (creek)

drift — to dig a tunnel sideways from the main vertical shaft once bedrock is reached

dump — gold bearing gravel dug out of the shaft and piled around its mouth

gold rush — a sudden migration of people to an area where gold has been found

goldfield — an area where gold has been found

gumboots — tall rubber boots

ingot — gold formed into a bar or other shape

The Klondike — the area drained by the creeks flowing into the Klondike River

lode — a vein in rock, usually quartz, containing metallic ore such as gold or silver

packers —people who charged a fee to carry loads along the Chilkoot Trail, especially over the Chilkoot Pass

panning — washing gravel in a pan to separate out the gold particles

pass — a gap (or notch) between two mountain peaks by which people and sometimes pack animals can cross a mountain range

paydirt — soil or gravel rich enough in gold to make mining profitable

paystreak — the seam of paydirt in the layer of gravel that covers the bedrock

placer — water-borne deposit of gravel or sand containing particles of mineral, especially gold, that can be washed out (pronounced "plasser")

poke — a small drawstring sack or bag made from canvas or moosehide, used to carry gold dust and nuggets

prospector — a person who searches for gold or other precious metals

roadhouse — a makeshift restaurant or hotel often located at the junction of two creeks

scow — a large, flat-bottomed boat with square ends

sourdough — fermented dough kept from one baking to the next to act as yeast in bread or biscuit making. Also, the nickname given someone who has spent a winter in the Klondike.

stampeder — a person who took part in the Klondike gold rush

tailings — the leftover sand and gravel after the gold has been removed

The Yukon — the area through which most of the Yukon River runs. On June 13, 1898, it entered Confederation as Yukon Territory.

INDEX